# HENRIK IBSEN

# Hedda Gabler

*translated by*
MICHAEL MEYER

*with commentary and notes by*
DAVID THOMAS

METHUEN DRAMA

**Methuen Drama Student Edition**

10 9 8 7 6 5

This edition first published in the United Kingdom in 2002
by Methuen Publishing Ltd

Methuen Drama
A & C Black Publishers Ltd
36 Soho Square
London W1D 3QY

Reissued with additional material and a new cover design 2005; reissued
with a new cover design 2009

This translation of *Hedda Gabler* first published in 1962
by Rupert Hart-Davis Ltd
and subsequently by Eyre Methuen in 1967
Revised edition published by Eyre Methuen in 1974
Copyright © 1962, 1974 by the Estate of Michael Meyer

Commentary and notes copyright © 2002, 2005 by David Thomas

The right of the authors to be identified as the authors of these works has
been asserted by them in accordance with the Copyright, Designs and
Patents Act, 1988

A CIP catalogue record for this book is available from the British Library

ISBN 978 0 413 77070 7

Cover Design Jocelyn Lucas
Cover Montage © Jocelyn Lucas 2009

Typeset by Deltatype Ltd, Birkenhead, Merseyside
Printed and bound in Great Britain by CPI Cox & Wyman,
Reading, Berkshire

**Caution**

# Contents

# Henrik Johan Ibsen:
# 1828–1906

1828 Henrik Johan Ibsen born in Skien on 20 March,
the second son of Knud Ibsen and his wife
Marichen (*née* Altenburg).

1835 Henrik's father, Knud Ibsen, a prosperous
merchant, is ruined financially as his business
empire collapses. The family moves out of town to
a property untouched by his creditors. The house
at Venstøp becomes the family home for the next
eight years. The whole family is deeply affected by
feelings of social humiliation. The experience of
these early years, and the physical environment of
the house, the attic and the surroundings at
Venstøp are reflected in many of Ibsen's later
plays.

1843 The family moves back to Skien from Venstøp in
October. Two months later Ibsen is sent to
Grimstad, a small town on the coast some sixty
miles to the south, to work as an apothecary's
apprentice. He remains in Grimstad for the next
six years and does not once visit his family during
this period of time.

1846 Ibsen fathers an illegitimate son with one of the
maids in the house, Else Sofie Jensen. He pays
paternity costs for the next fourteen years.

1848 Writes his first play *Catiline*, which is rejected by
–49  the Christiania Theatre.

1850 Travels to Christiania (now Oslo) to become a
student at the university. Visits his parents on the
way to the capital. This first visit home in six years
is not a success. After this visit, Ibsen makes a
decisive break with his parents and never sees
them or contacts them again. *Catiline* is published
privately under a pseudonym. Writes his second

play *The Warrior's Barrow* under the same
pseudonym. This is performed at the Christiania
Theatre in September.

1851 Invited by the famous violin player, Ole Bull, to
join the staff of his newly created National Theatre
in Bergen, Western Norway. Ibsen works there for
six years, as an associate director responsible for
movement, blocking and design. He is also
required to work as a dramatic author.

1852 Sent on a study tour to visit theatres in
Copenhagen, Hamburg and Dresden. Writes a
romantic comedy, *St John's Eve*.

1853 *St John's Eve* performed at Bergen, without success.

1854 A revised version of *The Warrior's Barrow* performed
at Bergen, without success.

1855 Writes a historical tragedy, *Lady Inger of Østraat*,
which is performed at Bergen, without success.
Writes a romantic comedy, *The Feast at Solhaug*.

1856 *The Feast at Solhaug* is his first real success when it
is performed in January. Meets Suzannah
Thoresen, his future wife. Writes *Olaf Liljekrans*,
another romantic comedy.

1857 *Olaf Liljekrans* is acted at Bergen, without success.
Ibsen leaves Bergen to take up a new post as
artistic director of the Norwegian Theatre in
Christiania. Writes *The Vikings at Helgeland*, a
historical tragedy.

1858 Marries Suzannah Thoresen. *The Vikings at Helgeland*
staged at the Norwegian Theatre in Christiania,
with modest success.

1859 His poem 'On the heights' is published in a
journal. His only child, Sigurd, is born.

1860 A period of poverty and despair. Ibsen is attacked
–61 in the press, drinks heavily and is unable to write.

1862 Writes *Love's Comedy*, a verse satire, his first play for
five years. It is rejected by his own theatre, which
goes bankrupt in June. Ibsen is now without a job.

1863 Appointed to a temporary job as a literary adviser
to the rival Christiania Theatre. Writes a major

historical tragedy, *The Pretenders*. Awarded a small
government grant to spend a study year in Rome.
This is augmented by a collection organised by
Bjørnson and other writers.

1864 *The Pretenders* performed successfully in Christiania.
Ibsen travels to Rome. He is to live abroad for the
next twenty-seven years.

1865 Writes his verse play, *Brand*, in Rome and Ariccia.
*Brand* is a magnificent dramatic poem, centred on
the life of a country priest who demands that
people give 'all or nothing' in their commitment to
God. The play explores the limits of human will-
power in the face of environmental and
psychological pressures and juxtaposes the demands
of vocation with those of love.

1866 *Brand* is published in Copenhagen and enjoys a
huge critical success in Scandinavia. Ibsen is
awarded an annual government grant to permit
him to concentrate on writing.

1867 Completes his verse play, *Peer Gynt*, while living in
Rome, Ischia and Sorrento. This too is critically
acclaimed. *Peer Gynt* explores many of the themes
addressed in *Brand*, but from a comic perspective.
Peer lives in a dream world he himself creates and
spends his life fleeing from any kind of
commitment. In the end he finds his real self in
the unconditional love of Solvejg, from whom he
once fled in terror.

1868 Moves from Rome and takes up permanent
residence in Dresden.

1869 Attends the opening of the Suez Canal as
Norway's official representative. Writes the comedy,
*The League of Youth*.

1870 Travels to Copenhagen for the summer months.

1871 Prepares an edition of his poems. From this point
onwards, he will write only in prose.

1873 Completes *Emperor and Galilean*, a dramatisation of
world-historical process that had taken nine years
to write. The play is above all concerned with the

quest for enlightenment of the Emperor Julian the Apostate.

1874 Visits Christiania for the first time in ten years. Students honour him with a torchlight procession.

1875 Leaves Dresden for Munich and begins work on *The Pillars of Society*.

1876 *Peer Gynt* staged for the first time with Grieg's music at the Christiana Theatre. *The Pretenders* performed in Berlin by the troupe of Duke George of Meiningen.

1877 Completes *The Pillars of Society*, which is acted with great success in leading German theatres. In this, his first great social play, Ibsen writes a barbed critique of the ruthless entrepreneurs who were introducing industrial capitalism into contemporary Norway.

1878 Returns to Rome for a year, visiting Gossensass en route.

1879 Writes *A Doll's House* in Rome and Amalfi. *A Doll's House* expresses a forceful indictment of contemporary middle-class marriage. Nora, the doll wife of the title, leaves her husband and her children at the end of the play to discover her real identity. The play provokes widespread debate and controversy in contemporary Europe and establishes Ibsen's international reputation.

1880 Moves back to Italy for a further five years.

1881 Writes *Ghosts* in Rome and Sorrento. *Ghosts* shows what happens when a woman, who has left her husband, is forced by social pressure to return. The result is a disastrous marriage that wrecks the lives of Mrs Alving, her husband and her son Osvald. The play is violently attacked by critics. Theatres refuse to perform it and booksellers return their copies to the publishers.

1882 Writes *An Enemy of the People* in Rome. This ironic social comedy is generally well received. The play depicts how the central character, Dr Stockman, is hounded by his local community for attempting to

publish details of pollution affecting a local spa.
There are obvious parallels between Stockman and
Ibsen. *Ghosts* is given its first stage performance in
Chicago.

1883 Writes *The Wild Duck* in Rome and Gossensass.

1884 *The Wild Duck* is published. There are echoes in
the play of Ibsen's own childhood at Venstøp. The
play shows how the fragile set of relationships,
binding together the Ekdal family, is wrecked by
the intervention of a neurotic outsider. Its blend of
tragic and comic effects causes consternation to
contemporary critics.

1885 Ibsen makes an extended visit to Norway for the
first time since 1874. He visits Trondheim, Molde,
Bergen and Kristiania (the spelling was changed
from Christiania in 1877). Moves from Rome to
Munich where he is to stay for the next six years.

1886 Writes *Rosmersholm* in Munich. The play contains
some echoes of his visit to Molde. In this complex
and subtle work, the major characters, Rebecca
West and John Rosmer, act out a drama of
thwarted and lethal passion that ends with their
suicide in a millrace. The play's ambiguities cause
bewilderment to contemporary critics.

1888 Writes *The Lady from the Sea* in Munich. This play
contains further echoes of his visit to Molde. The
action centres on the problems inherent in a
second marriage. Ellida Wangel feels trapped in
her marriage with a country doctor and alienated
from his two daughters. The play ends with a
sense of genuine reconciliation, albeit tinged with a
note of elegiac sadness.

1889 As in several previous years, spends the summer in
Gossensass. There he meets the young Emilie
Bardach, with whom he becomes infatuated.
Although they never meet again, they correspond
with each other for several months until Ibsen
terminates the correspondence in February 1890. *A
Doll's House*, with Janet Achurch in the lead role, is

given its first major production in London. Die
Freie Bühne in Berlin is launched with a
production of *Ghosts*.

1890 Writes *Hedda Gabler* in Munich. In this play, the
major character, Hedda Gabler, finds herself
trapped in a conventional marriage with a dull
middle-class husband and reacts violently to her
situation. The play's use of tragi-comic effects
causes dismay to Ibsen's contemporaries, and the
play is almost universally condemned. André
Antoine mounts a production of *Ghosts* at the
Théâtre Libre in Paris.

1891 J. T. Grein's Independent Theatre performs *Ghosts*
in London: the play is subjected to scathing
criticism. This is followed by a production of *Hedda
Gabler*, at the Vaudeville Theatre in London, which
is far more positively received. The success of this
production is largely due to the acting of Elizabeth
Robins in the title role. Ibsen takes a summer
holiday in Norway (a cruise to the North Cape), at
the end of which he decides to settle in Kristiania.
Moves into Victoria Terrasse.

1892 Writes *The Master Builder* in Kristiania. In this play,
Solness, a master builder, has exploited the young
people who work for him but he is now obsessed
with the threat of youth. He is finally driven to
prove his virile creativity to Hilde, a young
admirer, by climbing the high tower he himself has
designed. But he falls to his death. Ibsen's son
Sigurd marries Bergliot, daughter of the writer
Bjørnstjerne Bjørnson.

1894 Writes *Little Eyolf* in Kristiania. In this complex
work, Ibsen shows the marriage between Rita and
Alfred Allmers being undermined by Alfred's
incestuous fantasies involving his half-sister, Asta.

1895 Moves from Victoria Terrasse to Arbiensgate, on
the corner with Drammensvejen.

1896 Writes *John Gabriel Borkman* in Kristiania. Further
memories of Ibsen's own unhappy childhood are

reflected in this play, set in a bleak winter
landscape. Borkman, a former industrial magnate,
has served a prison sentence for speculating with
money belonging to others. He also sacrificed the
woman he loved for the sake of his career. The
play traces out the human consequences of his
ruthless ambition.

1898 Ibsen receives congratulations from all over the
world on his seventieth birthday. He also receives
honours and decorations. Publication is begun on
his collected works in Norwegian and German.

1899 Writes *When We Dead Awaken* in Kristiania. In this
play, Ibsen yet again explores the conflicting
demands of art and life, vocation and personal
happiness. The ageing sculptor Rubek is confronted
in the play by Irene, the youthful model who
inspired his early work. He once rejected her for
the sake of material gain, but he now commits
himself to her in a work that has the mythical
quality of a dream play.

1900 Ibsen suffers a first stroke, which leaves him unable
to write.

1901 Suffers a further stroke, which leaves him largely
paralysed and helpless.

1906 Ibsen dies in Kristiania on 23 May, aged seventy-
eight.

# Plot

The play is divided into four acts. The setting remains
the same throughout the action, namely a large drawing-
room in the villa of George [Jørgen] Tesman and his
wife Hedda. In the rear wall, a broad open doorway
leads to a smaller room, decorated in the same style as
the drawing-room. This is Hedda's private room, which
is dominated by a portrait of her late father, General
Gabler. The right-hand wall of the drawing-room
contains a folding door to the hall. On the opposite wall
there are french windows looking out over a veranda
and a garden, with trees in autumn colours. The room is
tastefully furnished with elegant sofas, chairs, and tables.
There is a piano and a large tiled stove. The whole
action of the play takes place within a compressed
timeframe, reminiscent of a neo-classic play. It begins in
the early morning and is completed during the evening
of the following day.

*Act One*
When the play opens, George Tesman and his wife
Hedda have returned the previous evening to their newly
acquired town villa after a honeymoon abroad lasting
almost six months. Tesman's aunt, Juliana [Juliane]
Tesman, whom he calls Auntie Juju, pays an early-
morning call to welcome the couple home with a bunch
of flowers. Bertha [Berte], the maid, is the first person
she meets. Previously, Bertha was Miss Tesman's maid;
both of them regret this change. However, Miss Tesman
felt that George would not be able to manage without
Bertha, as he had relied on her assistance since his
boyhood. There is a close bond between Miss Tesman
and Bertha. Both of them are a little concerned that

Hedda has such different tastes and expectations from
their own. For instance, she has even removed the chintz
covers from the furniture in the drawing-room.

When George Tesman enters, he very clearly shares
the same values as his aunt and Bertha. He begins by
apologising shamefacedly to his aunt for not giving her a
lift home from the ferry terminal at midnight, as he and
Hedda had too much luggage with them. He then
welcomes his aunt with real affection and admires the
new hat she has bought for her future walks with
Hedda.

Auntie Juju wants to know if there is any happy event
in the offing. However, George is so obtuse that he fails
to grasp what she is referring to. They then talk briefly
of all the money that has been spent on the honeymoon
and on acquiring Tesman's splendid villa, the home of
the former Prime Minister's widow. To his horror,
Tesman learns that his aunt has taken out a mortgage
on her annuity (her pension income) in order to meet
the initial costs. It seems that their friend Judge Brack,
who made the detailed arrangements, assured her that
this was only a formality. Briefly, they mention Tesman's
former professional rival, Eilert Loevborg [Ejlert
Løvborg], who has apparently published a new book.

When Hedda enters, she is in an angry mood. She
has almost certainly been eavesdropping on the
conversation between her husband and his beloved aunt.
Hedda dislikes the light flooding into the room through
the french windows, which Bertha had opened. She feels
even greater dislike for the cosy, sentimental relationship
between Tesman and his aunt. When Tesman attempts
to force her to take an interest in his old slippers, which
Auntie Juju has brought with her, Hedda explodes.
Instead of attacking Tesman or his aunt directly, she
directs her fury at Auntie Juju's new hat. She pointedly
accuses Bertha of having left her old hat on the chair.
Tesman is appalled and his aunt is deeply offended.
However, when Tesman attempts to smooth things over
and comments on the way Hedda has 'filled out', his

aunt melts. He has no idea of what is implied in his
statement, but his aunt does. Miss Tesman takes her
farewell, blessing Hedda, for George's sake. While
Tesman sees out his aunt, Hedda clenches her fists in
furious frustration. After Tesman's return to the stage,
Hedda confesses that she insulted Miss Tesman's hat
deliberately. She promises to make amends by inviting
her to afternoon tea. However, she refuses to call her
Auntie Juju: Aunt Juliana is as far as she is prepared to
go.

Another visitor is now announced, Mrs Thea Elvsted.
Hedda apparently knew her at school, and was greatly
irritated by her fine head of hair, which, according to
Hedda, Thea was always showing off. It also seems that
she was an old flame of Tesman's. Both of them, but
especially Hedda, are curious about the reason for her
visit to town. Mrs Elvsted is obviously agitated, but is
cautious about revealing the real reason for her concern.
Clearly it has something to do with Eilert Loevborg who
has tutored her husband's children for the past few
years. She confirms that Loevborg has recently published
a new book on the history of civilisation, which has
created quite a stir. But she is worried that he may
succumb to temptation now that he is back in town. She
asks Tesman to be kind to Loevborg and to keep an eye
on him. Hedda sends Tesman out to write a note to
Loevborg so that she can extract more information from
Mrs Elvsted.

Under Hedda's probing inquisition, Mrs Elvsted
confesses that her five-year marriage to Elvsted, a
country magistrate, has been deeply unhappy. Twenty
years older than her, he has shown her little
consideration and even less affection. In contrast, Eilert
Loevborg has played an increasingly important role in
her life. He has shared his thoughts and ideas with her
and in return she has given him the stability he needed
to write a new book. They worked together like close
friends. But now Eilert has come back to town and she
is worried that there is a shadow of another woman

between them: a woman who once threatened him with
a pistol. She has decided to burn her boats, to leave her
husband and her empty marriage, in order to live where
Eilert Loevborg is. Hedda is shocked at Mrs Elvsted's
open defiance of convention, but promises to keep to
herself what Thea has told her. When Tesman re-
appears with his note for Eilert, Judge Brack's arrival is
announced. Hedda offers to accompany Thea through
the garden after she has briefly greeted Judge Brack.

This first time Brack and Hedda meet on stage, there
is a discernible sense of pleasurable flirtation between
them. However, Judge Brack has come to bring some
disturbing news to the Tesmans. It seems that Eilert is
now determined to offer himself as a candidate for the
chair to which Tesman had hoped to be appointed. He
had married and borrowed money to purchase his villa
on the expectation of a professorial appointment. Now,
with the prospect of a competition with Loevborg,
nothing seems certain. Initially, Hedda claims to be
unconcerned. Indeed, she quite likes the idea of a
competition: it seems to her like a duel. Judge Brack
suggests with ironic detachment that she may
nevertheless have to restrain her urge to make expensive
new purchases. As soon as Brack leaves, Tesman
reiterates Brack's warning and makes it clear to Hedda
that her hopes of a footman, a bay mare and elegant
parties must now be put on hold. Hedda responds to his
threat with one of her own. At least she still has her
father's pistols to keep her entertained.

## Act Two

It is now late afternooon. Hedda is in the process of
implementing the threat she made at the end of Act
One. She is loading one of General Gabler's pistols and
shoots it at Judge Brack who is coming through the
garden, the back way into the house. After entering
through the french windows, Brack relieves Hedda of her
pistol and locks it away in its case. They sit close to

each other and continue the same pattern of flirtation they began in the morning. Hedda confesses that she has been utterly bored throughout her honeymoon and finds her husband's obsession with his special subject tedious beyond measure. Brack asks why she married Tesman, if she finds him so dreary. She obviously felt that she was in danger of remaining unmarried as no one of her own class, least of all Brack, was willing to offer to wed her. Brack confesses that he is averse to marrying and instead far prefers comfortable triangular relationships with a married couple where he can be a friend of the husband and an even closer friend of the wife. Hedda's response to this suggestion is ambiguous. She is not willing to jump off the marriage train, but she is prepared to welcome a trusted friend into her compartment.

After a brief interruption, when Tesman arrives home carrying a stack of books and then disappears to change into evening dress, Hedda continues her conversation with Brack. She admits that she was rude to Auntie Juju and that when a sudden mood like that overtakes her, she cannot stop herself. She goes on to confess that she does not even like the splendid house they live in. She only pretended to like it one evening when Tesman was walking her home in order to make polite conversation. In fact she dislikes the house intensely with its smell of lavender and dried roses; for her, it has the odour of death. She sees a life of boredom stretching out in front of her. If Tesman had a socially attractive position in politics, she could at least have some fun. But their lack of money and Tesman's lack of ability make life seem hateful to her. When Brack probes her on her attitude to motherhood, her mood darkens discernibly.

Following this quiet and thoughtful opening, the act now moves into a different rhythm. Tesman returns in his evening dress, ready for Brack's dinner party. Shortly afterwards, all three are joined by Loevborg. Tesman congratulates Loevborg on his new book. Loevborg brushes aside these kind words and shows the manuscript of his latest work. This apparently is the book where he

has spoken with his real voice: it is a book about the
forces that will shape society in future. Brack invites
Loevborg to join them at his dinner party. At this stage,
Loevborg declines, preferring to stay and have supper
with Hedda and Mrs Elvsted (who has yet to arrive).
Loevborg then goes on to state that he will give a series
of lectures on his new book during the autumn.
However, he will not challenge Tesman for the chair.
He only wants to defeat Tesman in the eyes of the
world. Tesman, who is not interested in honour but only
in his future prospects, is overjoyed.

Hedda now ushers Brack and Tesman into her
upstage private room to drink cold punch and smoke
cigarettes before leaving for Brack's dinner party.
Loevborg, who is clearly a former alcoholic, declines to
join them. Instead, he remains with Hedda who offers to
show him photographs of the Tyrol which she and
Tesman visited at the end of their honeymoon. This
suggestion provides them with perfect cover to have a
more intimate conversation. Loevborg grasps the
opportunity, asking Hedda how she could throw herself
away on a man like Tesman. At which point, Tesman
joins them to ask Hedda if she would also like some
punch. Hedda and Loevborg continue their conversation,
which is punctuated by a further visit from Tesman and
which is keenly observed at a distance by Brack. In a
few brief lines, they trace out their past relationship.
Loevborg used to visit Hedda and sit with her in the
same room as General Gabler. But while the General
read his newspapers, Loevborg talked to Hedda about
his dissipated life and she asked him probing questions.
Eventually, Loevborg made a pass at her and she
apparently threatened to shoot him. She now confesses
that her failure to shoot him was not her greatest act of
cowardice that evening. This is the closest she comes to
confessing her love for Loevborg and she immediately
denies the significance of what she has just said. At the
very moment when these two are reliving their most
intense experiences, Thea Elvsted arrives.

Hedda now takes decisive action to wreck the cosy relationship of trust that Thea and Loevborg have built up. Initially she tries to tempt Loevborg into drinking a glass of cold punch. When he refuses, she turns sweetly to Thea and comments that Thea's worries about Loevborg that morning are completely unfounded. He is obviously a man of firm principle. Her comment has the desired effect. Loevborg realises that Thea's trust in him was after all somewhat thin. In his anger, he quickly downs two glasses of punch. He then accepts Brack's invitation to join him for his gentlemen's dinner party. He assures Thea that he will come back to see her home at ten o'clock.

After the men have gone, Thea Elvsted is left with a feeling of deep anxiety. In contrast, Hedda feels elated that she has at last had the power, as she puts it, to shape a man's destiny. She sees Loevborg returning in triumph with vine leaves in his hair. The image is so intoxicating that she feels like burning off Thea's hair. Instead, she drags her away to tea in the dining-room.

*Act Three*

When Act Three opens, Thea and Hedda have waited in vain all night for the men to return home. It is now seven o'clock in the morning and there is still no sign of them. The women have tried to sleep in an armchair or on the sofa, but without much success. Hedda wants Thea out of the way in case the men do arrive back with interesting tales to tell. She insists that Thea go to her bedroom and try to sleep properly.

Soon after, Tesman enters on tiptoes and is astonished to find Hedda already up. Tesman soon tells her the tale of what happened at Brack's party. It all started well enough, with Loevborg reading to Tesman from his brilliant new book before the other guests arrived. However, when the party began in earnest, Loevborg, it seems, reverted to his old ways and ended up completely drunk. Tesman and others offered to see Loevborg

home, as he was in no state to make his own way from
Brack's house. As they walked along, Tesman fell back
to relieve himself and found that Loevborg had
accidentally dropped his precious manuscript by the
roadside. Because of Loevborg's drunken state, Tesman
did not dare to return the manuscript to him. Loevborg
and several others then disappeared on the outskirts of
town and Tesman ended up drinking coffee with another
group of Brack's guests.

After this account of the night's events, Hedda asks to
read the manuscript. Tesman declines to give it to her;
he feels that he should return it at once. At this point,
he is distracted by a letter from Auntie Juju summoning
him to the deathbed of his other aunt, Auntie Rena
[Rina]. He dashes off, leaving Hedda to bundle the
manuscript into her writing desk, as Judge Brack is
announced.

Brack has come to complete the narrative of the
night's events and to spell out their consequences to
Hedda. It seems that Loevborg did not go home, after
giving Tesman the slip, but instead ended up in an
establishment run by a red-headed singer, Mademoiselle
Danielle [Diana]. Loevborg had been one of her most
loyal patrons in the old days. Last night, her initial
warm welcome soon turned to acrimony as he began to
accuse her and her friends of robbing him of his pocket-
book (his manuscript). Eventually, the police were called
and Loevborg caused even more trouble by violently
resisting arrest. Brack now informs Hedda that, because
of this disgrace, all doors will in future be shut to
Loevborg and Thea Elvsted. Hedda must follow suit and
do likewise. He takes obvious pleasure in the prospect of
Loevborg being excluded from Hedda's circle. Brack
admits that his aim is to be cock of the walk. He also
admits that he would fight for this position with every
weapon at his disposal. For the first time, Hedda realises
that Brack would be dangerous if he had any kind of
hold over her. Once again Brack leaves by the back
door, commenting that back doors can be intriguing.

Immediately after Brack's exit, there is a commotion in the hall, Loevborg forces his way in, past Bertha, to see Hedda. The noise wakes Thea Elvsted. Loevborg announces his intention of breaking off his relationship with Thea. In his view, he would simply drag her down, if she were to remain associated with him. To make the break irrevocable, he lies to her and claims that he destroyed the manuscript of the book she had helped him to write, scattering the pieces in the fjord. In anguish, Thea says that it feels like Loevborg has killed a child, their child. Empty and distraught, she leaves Loevborg and Hedda to face an uncertain future.

Loevborg now confesses the truth to Hedda, namely that he lost his manuscript during the previous night's heavy drinking. Again he stresses the parallel between the manuscript and a child. Filled with self-loathing, he wants to put an end to it all. Instead of returning his manuscript to him, Hedda asks Loevborg to kill himself beautifully. She gives him one of her father's pistols, the same pistol with which she once threatened him. After Loevborg's departure, Hedda takes out his manuscript and burns it in the stove page by page. As she does so, she whispers that she is burning Thea's child, the child Eilert Loevborg had given her.


## Act Four

The final act opens in the darkness of late evening. Hedda is dressed in black, and is shortly joined by Miss Tesman who is dressed in mourning. Auntie Rena has passed away. Hedda receives Miss Tesman politely, but studiously avoids expressing her condolences. Miss Tesman drops several hints about Hedda's pregnancy, but Hedda equally studiously ignores these. George Tesman now arrives home, and his aunt leaves to make the arrangements for Auntie Rena's burial shortly afterwards. Tesman is in a state of considerable agitation. He is naturally upset at the death of his Auntie Rena, but is even more concerned about Loevborg's state of

mind. His main aim is to return Loevborg's manuscript to him in case Loevborg does anything desperate. At this point, Hedda drops her bolt from the blue and confesses coldly that she burned Loevborg's precious manuscript.

Not for the first time in his relationship with Hedda, Tesman finds himself emotionally out of his depth. However, Hedda proceeds to handle this particular crisis with consummate skill. Once George has recovered from his initial shock, Hedda suggests to him that she burned Loevborg's manuscript because she could not bear the thought of anyone pushing her husband into the shade. Tesman begins to melt at the thought of Hedda showing him even the slightest sign of affection. She then goes on to hint at her pregnancy, which produces a response of boyish euphoria in Tesman. Indeed, he is so overjoyed at the news that he wants to run out of the room to tell the maid Bertha, who has obviously been his confidante since his childhood. This response threatens to ignite a further explosion of rage in Hedda at the prospect of being implicated in the web of maudlin sentimentality that binds Tesman together with Auntie Juju and Bertha. As always, the mere threat of an uncontrolled outburst on Hedda's part is sufficient to bring Tesman to heel. He agrees that it would not be appropriate to say anything to Bertha, but he will instead tell Auntie Juju. Meanwhile, he accepts the burning of Loevborg's manuscript as a price worth paying for Hedda's affection. Clearly Tesman's set of moral principles proves infinitely pliable when it comes to his own personal advantage.

Their conversation is interrupted by the arrival of Mrs Elvsted. She is beside herself with anxiety. Eilert has not returned to his lodgings and no one will tell her what has happened; however, she overheard people talking about him being in hospital. At this point, Judge Brack arrives to announce that Loevborg is indeed dying in hospital. Hedda guesses correctly that Loevborg has shot himself. Brack confirms that this is the case; Loevborg has shot himself in the breast. He watches Hedda

intently as she not only guesses Loevborg's fate but claims that there is something beautiful in the way he has settled his account with life. Tesman and Mrs Elvsted disagree with her; from their more prosaic perspective, Loevborg must have been desperate and mad to shoot himself. Tesman, for good reason, is saddened at the thought of Loevborg dying without leaving behind him his new work, the one thing that would have made his name endure. At this point, Mrs Elvsted reveals that she still has Loevborg's notes for his new book: she carries them with her in her dress pocket, almost as a memento of their former creative partnership. Tesman is delighted at this news and offers to work with her to piece together a version of Loevborg's manuscript. He claims that he owes this to Eilert's memory, but it is obvious that for him this offers a perfect opportunity to assuage his guilt over the burning of Eilert's manuscript. They move into Hedda's private room to begin their work, leaving Hedda alone with Brack.

Brack begins his dialogue with Hedda by disabusing her of any false illusions concerning Loevborg's death. Far from being a noble and beautiful deed, it was a sordid accident that happened when Loevborg had returned to Mademoiselle Danielle's establishment to search yet again for his lost manuscript. The pistol he was carrying in his breast pocket went off and he was shot in the genitals. Hedda recoils in revulsion from this prospect; it is as if everything she touches seems to degenerate into something mean and ludicrous. Brack continues with what sounds increasingly like an interrogation. He turns to the issue of the pistol Loevborg had in his breast pocket. Without giving any description of the pistol, he suggests that it must have been stolen. Hedda falls into this simple trap and denies that Loevborg stole the pistol. In so doing, she confirms her involvement in Loevborg's possession of a pistol.

Brack and Hedda are interrupted as Tesman and Mrs Elvsted move to Hedda's writing desk where the light is

better. Before they install themselves, Hedda removes
things (including her pistol) from her desk into her
private room. Brack then continues his inquisition with
renewed vigour. He tells Hedda that he recognised the
pistol with which Loevborg had shot himself as soon as
the police showed it to him: it was one of the two pistols
that Hedda had inherited from her father. So far Brack
has not informed the police of this. But if the owner is
traced, then Hedda will be faced by the scandal of a
court case involving Mademoiselle Danielle. In court she
will have to explain why, if Loevborg did not steal the
pistol, she gave it to him. Brack makes it very clear that
none of this need happen if he holds his tongue. Hedda
now realises that Brack has her entirely in his power.
She finds that thought unbearable.

Mockingly she asks Tesman and Mrs Elvsted how
their labours are progressing, and comments ironically
that Thea will soon inspire her husband as she once did
Eilert Loevborg. She withdraws into her private room
and draws the curtains. In an act of childish petulance,
she plays a loud dance tune on her piano and is at once
silenced by her husband. Tesman now suggests that Mrs
Elvsted should move in with Auntie Juju and that, in
future, he should spend the evenings with her at his
aunt's house, trying to piece together Loevborg's notes.
He also suggests to Brack that he should come over and
keep Hedda company. Brack is of course delighted at the
prospect and already looks forward to the fun he and
Hedda will have together. Hedda comments venomously
from her room that it would suit him perfectly to be the
only cock on the dunghill. And at that she shoots herself.
Tesman pulls open the curtains to reveal Hedda lying
dead on the sofa. Both he and Brack comment
incongruously on Hedda's unexpected and
disproportionate gesture of defiance.

# Commentary

## The biographical and historical context

In the summer of 1889 Ibsen met a young girl from
Vienna called Emilie Bardach. At the time both of them
were on holiday in the South Tyrolean village called
Gossensass (Colle Isarco). Emilie Bardach was a young
débutante, a mere eighteen years old: Ibsen was an
internationally famous writer in his early sixties. During
the two months or so they spent in Gossensass they met
frequently and gradually became infatuated with each
other. At the end of the summer, Ibsen returned to
Munich and Emilie to Vienna. They wrote frequent
letters to each other, with a shimmering subtext beneath
the carefully chosen words, until Ibsen broke off the
correspondence in February 1890.

Behind these bare facts lies the emotional starting
point for *Hedda Gabler* and the remainder of Ibsen's late
plays. In her youthfulness Emilie represented spontaneous
experience, the very thing that Ibsen had sacrificed in
pursuit of his art. For the sake of 'the power and the
glory' Ibsen had long ago renounced any kind of
emotional spontaneity, choosing instead to fetter his
emotions in iron bands of self-control. If need be, he was
prepared to ride roughshod over his own feelings and
those of others. All of this, Emilie, 'light, quick, poised
like a bird, gracious in velvet and furs . . .',*
threatened to undermine and destroy. The summer
months he spent with her in Gossensass made him
painfully aware of the lack of emotional fulfilment in his
own life. After returning to Munich he was evidently

* Writing to Emilie on 22 December 1889, this is how Ibsen said he saw
her, walking along the Ringstrasse. This and the following descriptions
of her are quoted from M. Meyer, *Ibsen: A Biography*, pp. 645–54.

disturbed and torn by his relationship with her. She
represented the joy of life, the very thing he valued and
praised as an artist. But she brought her spontaneity into
his life at a point when it was too late for him to be
able to respond to her with matching warmth. He called
her 'the May sun of a September life'. There was also
another feature in their relationship that greatly troubled
Ibsen. Emilie was not only young and beautiful, she was
also bored and spoilt. With 'a tired look' in her
'mysterious eyes', she seemed to him, on reflection,
rather like a bird of prey who took delight in capturing
other women's husbands. Her lack of purpose in life
made her potentially dangerous and destructive. Ibsen
gradually came to realise that Emilie probably needed
him more than he needed her, and that her needs could
only be met at the price of considerable emotional havoc
and destruction. As this realisation became increasingly
clear, Ibsen, with his usual instinct for self-preservation,
decided to terminate the relationship.

By February of 1890 he was also deeply immersed in
the preparatory work for a new play. To have prolonged
the relationship with Emilie any further would have
disturbed the concentration he needed to work and
would have therefore involved a tacit acceptance that life
was indeed more important than art. It was one thing to
dream of emotional fulfilment and quite another to try
and achieve it. Shortly before they parted in Gossensass,
Ibsen, with prophetic clarity, had written in Emilie's
album a line from Goethe's *Faust*: 'Hohes, schmerzliches
Glück – um das Unerreichbare zu ringen!' [Oh, high
and painful joy – to struggle for the unattainable!]
(Meyer, p. 639). Even then he knew what would happen
when he finally had to make the choice between art and
life; it would take more than one summer in Gossensass
to make him relinquish the power and the glory. But
neither his art nor his life would ever be quite the same
again. The mood of elegiac renunciation and sadness
towards which he had seemed to be moving in *The Lady
from the Sea* gave way, in his new play *Hedda Gabler*, to a

sense of frustration, bitterness and disappointment. As
Ibsen depicted it in *Hedda Gabler*, life was a savage farce;
but, like the heroine of his play, he was determined to
treat it with aristocratic contempt. After Gossensass,
Ibsen seems to have concluded that his emotional life
would remain stunted but in *Hedda Gabler* he showed his
determination to have the last laugh at life's cruel
ironies.

To begin with, Ibsen's work on the play progressed
painfully and slowly. He obviously found it difficult to
place himself at sufficient distance from his material to
give it artistic shape and form. But gradually an outline
began to emerge. From the extensive draft material that
has survived for this play, one can observe Ibsen
moulding his recent experiences into an artistically
cohesive whole. Echoes of Gossensass recur frequently.
(In the play itself the village is mentioned, if not by
name, at least by location when Hedda looks at the
photograph album with Loevborg in Act Two.) There
are snatches of conversation in his notes that come
straight from his own interaction with Emilie. Hedda,
like Emilie, is intelligent but bored. She would dearly like
to influence someone else's life and is particularly excited
at the thought of stealing someone else's lover or
husband. In Ibsen's notes, Hedda even looks like Emilie.
She is described as having, an 'aristocratically formed
elegant face with fine wax-coloured skin. Eyes with a
veiled expression'.* The demonic poet figure in the
play, Eilert Loevborg, expresses, in Ibsen's notes, ideas
that were dear to Ibsen's own heart. And there is every
reason to suppose, from the evidence of Emilie's diary,
that Ibsen had in fact expressed similar thoughts to her
(see Meyer, pp. 636–8). Ibsen, like Loevborg, wanted to
find a way 'towards a companionship between man and
woman, whereby the true spiritual individual may
emerge' (*Oxford Ibsen*, vol. vii, p. 487). (He had already
explored this notion in his earlier play, *Rosmersholm*.) It

* All quotations from Ibsen's notes to *Hedda Gabler* are from the *Oxford
Ibsen*, vol. vii, pp. 476–97.

requires little imagination to see him talking to Emilie
when Loevborg says in the notes:

> When I had thrown off this new book, another great and
> brilliant work emerged before me. And you must help me
> with it. I need women, Hedda – !

> Cannot a man be friends with several men, and then why
> not also with several women?

However, Ibsen's notes also show him moving well
beyond the limits of his actual experiences in Gossensass,
transforming them into quite different outcomes.
Loevborg, for instance, even at this early stage in Ibsen's
planning, was destined to come to a flamboyant and
violent end. Ibsen's quickly re-asserted self-control
ensured that he would never share a similar fate.
Perhaps Loevborg was something of a warning to himself
about the consequences of giving in to spontaneous
emotions. The Ibsen of everyday reality bore more
resemblance to the bourgeois academic George Tesman,
Hedda's husband, whom Ibsen describes with
considerable scorn even in his notes. Like Tesman, Ibsen
was better at coping with ideas and thoughts, carefully
ordering and structuring them, than he was at coping
with real experience. Perhaps the amount of scorn that
Ibsen poured on Tesman was in effect a subconscious
acknowledgement of his own pusillanimity in his dealings
with Emilie.

In addition to such direct and oblique echoes from
Gossensass, Ibsen's notes indicate how his recent personal
experiences were to be only the starting point for a play
about men and women interacting within the limitations
imposed by contemporary bourgeois society. Although
Ibsen was later to claim that *Hedda Gabler* was never
intended to be a problem play, his notes make it
perfectly clear that it was conceived as a social play, a
play in which social conditioning and social expectations
thwart and inhibit human potentiality.

The title of the play is quite significant. Originally
Ibsen had thought of calling it *Hedda*, but eventually

decided on calling it *Hedda Gabler* for reasons he
explained in a letter to his French translator:

> The title of the play is: *Hedda Gabler*. I intended to indicate
> thereby that as a personality she is to be regarded rather as
> her father's daughter than as her husband's wife. (*Oxford
> Ibsen*, vol. vii, p. 500)

Hedda's father was a general in the Norwegian army,
which gave him a status akin to that of a high-ranking
aristocrat. Although the aristocracy as such was abolished
in Norway in 1821, military and top administrative
families continued to play and indeed act out the role of
a privileged élite during the remainder of the century.
During the early 1890s, there were only eleven generals
in the Norwegian army, apart from the King and Crown
Prince. From Ibsen's notes we learn that General Gabler
was already an old man when Hedda was born and that
he eventually left the army, having fallen into some
disfavour. The prestige and attention Hedda had enjoyed
while her father was still a general was in marked
contrast to the sense of social embarrassment and even
exclusion she had felt after he had retired, or had been
retired, from the army.

The gossip, the oblique comments, even the tactful
silences, would have been unbearable. No wonder Hedda
fled from the glittering but merciless world of high
society in which she had grown up to the safe, if boring,
domesticity of a marriage with a dull, bourgeois
academic. These two contrasting worlds are summed up
in the play itself by Judge Brack, who represents the
values of her old social circle, and George Tesman and
his Auntie Juju who embody the values of middle-class
domesticity.

Brack had been Hedda's escort during her golden
years as a ballroom belle, but had turned his attention
elsewhere, possibly after her father's disgrace. Brack,
whose Norwegian title is 'Assessor', belongs like General
Gabler to a privileged élite in society. As an Assessor
(the term went out of use in 1927), he would have

served as a judge in one of three courts: the City Court, the Court of Appeal or the High Court. All of these were collegiate courts, presided over by panels of judges whose powers and discretion were considerable. Norway had no jury system in the 1890s. Brack's standing in society was therefore substantial. As befits his social position, he is a thoroughgoing pragmatist: a man of the world, always impeccably polite, charming and witty, but utterly ruthless in pursuit of his own advantage.

In contrast to Brack, Hedda's husband, George Tesman, comes from less exalted circles. Having been orphaned at an early age, he was brought up by two maiden aunts, Juliana and Rena, within their kindly but sentimental and ultimately self-indulgent environment. Auntie Juju's kindliness and compassion are highly selective and carefully calculated to meet her own spiritual needs. Underneath her soft exterior, there is a selfish and possessive streak in her. Ibsen comments in his notes, 'Hedda is right about this: There is no love on Tesman's side. Nor on the aunt's either. However loving she may be'. Clever and hard-working, Tesman grew up a pampered, protected but ambitious young man. Despite his bourgeois tastes and lack of *savoir faire*, he is just about acceptable to Hedda, in social terms, as a potential husband in as far as he has prospects of being elected to a chair at the university. In the 1890s the title of Professor still enjoyed a certain cachet in Norwegian society and the position brought with it secure and generous financial emoluments. Hedda can therefore envisage marriage with Tesman as a possible solution to her dilemma. Tesman may be ridiculous but his position in society will at least ensure Hedda some standing and, unlike Brack, he is neither dangerous nor devious.

Of the other characters in the play, the maidservant Bertha clearly belongs within the same social sphere as Tesman and his aunts. Although a maidservant, rather than a member of the bourgeoisie, she nevertheless shares the same social attitudes and aspirations as Tesman's aunts who were her former employers. Ibsen

himself pointed this out in a letter to Kristine Steen:

> George Tesman, his old aunts, and the elderly serving maid
> Bertha together form a whole and a unity. They have a
> common way of thinking; common memories, and a
> common attitude to life. For Hedda, they appear as an
> inimical and alien power directed against her fundamental
> nature. For this reason, there must be harmony between
> them in performance. (Letter to Kristine Steen, 14 January
> 1891. *Oxford Ibsen*, vol. vii, p. 505)

In complete contrast, Eilert Loevborg and, through him,
Thea Elvsted have rejected the normal limitations
imposed by bourgeois society and have established a
relationship based on notions of non-marital
companionship. Both share the same social status of
having worked as, respectively, a governess and a tutor
in a wealthy household, a county sheriff's family. But
they differ in as far as Thea originally comes from
Tesman's bourgeois environment and would dearly love
a cosy and respectable home. Whereas Loevborg is an
aristocrat of the mind who finds the realities of
contemporary bourgeois society repulsive and
constraining. Consequently, he finds himself driven all
too easily into excess and debauchery. Already in Ibsen's
early notes for the play, Loevborg comments on this
aspect of his character:

> I am not fundamentally dissipated. But real life isn't liveable
> – Why should I follow a social morality that I know cannot
> last another half generation. When I am licentious, as they
> call it, it is a flight from the present. Not because I get any
> pleasure out of licentiousness. I am too strongly rooted in
> this age for that.
>
> Thea, that little idiot, doesn't understand anything about it.
> But she's delicious all the same. There is an unconscious
> futurity in her.

These are the figures who act out Ibsen's tragicomedy
*Hedda Gabler*. At times the action is closer to black farce
than tragedy. Again in his preliminary notes Ibsen

anticipates this mood in a brief description he gives of Hedda's state of mind, 'Life for Hedda resolves itself as a farce that isn't worth seeing through to the end' (*Oxford Ibsen*, vol. vii, p. 486). And this farcical quality she sees colours everything that is said and done in the play, reducing even the most poetic ideals to a mockery of themselves. During the action serious things happen and eventually both Loevborg and Hedda die. The potential wasted in these two deaths is clearly tragic in substance. But the manner of their deaths and the reaction their deaths produce in others are essentially comic. The play even closes on a 'laugh' line, with Brack's totally incongruous response to Hedda's histrionic suicide, 'But, good God! People don't do such things!'

The predominantly comic tone of the play is reinforced by a simple linear structure. Ibsen's tragedies *Ghosts* and *Rosmersholm* depend for their effect on a retrospective analytic structure, allowing characters to explore how their past experiences have shaped their current responses. In contrast, the action of *Hedda Gabler* moves forward in a linear manner and pays only fleeting attention to the past. The dialogue is highly compressed, as it is in comic writing. There are no long passages of analytic dialogue. The speeches are short in length and there are frequent comic exchanges and misunder- standings. Even the structural pattern adopted by Ibsen is more appropriate to a comedy than a tragedy. Each act builds towards a climax, in which Hedda is seen to react with varying degrees of comic or spiteful exaggeration to her situation.

Hedda's reactions may be summarised as follows: At the end of Act One she is faced by the possibility that Tesman may fail to obtain the professorial position on which he had counted. This would mean the threat of social and financial regression and Hedda would no longer be able to have a footman, to purchase a bay mare and to hold elegant parties in her new home. She reacts to this prospect by threatening to amuse herself with her father's pistols. At the end of Act Two, having

effectively destroyed Loevborg's relationship of trust with Thea, Hedda goads Loevborg into drinking and then into joining the men at Brack's dinner party, instead of staying meekly behind with Hedda and Thea, as might befit a reformed alcoholic. Loevborg is sent forth by Hedda with the injunction to return with vine leaves in his hair. This prospect fills Hedda with such jubilation that she feels like burning off Thea's hair. At the end of Act Three, Loevborg threatens to take his life after the disgrace and humiliation of the previous night's events. Hedda asks him to die nobly and gives him one of General Gabler's pistols, the same pistol with which she had once threatened him. In sending Loevborg out to die, Hedda not only hopes to inspire him to an act of aristocratic heroism; she is also ensuring that Loevborg will no longer belong to Thea Elvsted. The relationship of these two engenders feelings of violent jealousy in her. She now vents all the anger she feels at this cosy relationship between Loevborg and Thea by burning Thea's 'child': the manuscript of the book, which Loevborg wrote under Thea's calming influence. By the end of Act Four, in much the same way as she once inspired Loevborg to reform, Thea has begun to inspire Hedda's husband, Tesman, to work with her on Loevborg's notes. Brack also pressures Hedda into admitting that she gave Loevborg the pistol with which he was shot. She can only avoid scandal if Brack remains silent. Brack now has her in his power. By the end of the play, Hedda is both trapped and rejected. In response, she shoots herself in a gesture of dispropor-tionate defiance.

Hedda herself admits that she cannot control her own responses when a sudden mood comes over her. However, the exaggerated nature of her responses takes the other characters by surprise. Hedda's extreme and inappropriate behaviour also provokes laughter on the part of an audience. Despite the seriousness of the issues addressed in the action, the predominant tone is one of comic incongruity. Not surprisingly, *Hedda Gabler*

totally mystified most of Ibsen's contemporaries. Even
enthusiastic admirers of Ibsen's work either failed to
understand what Ibsen meant or, if they had any inkling
of what was happening in the play, strongly disliked
what they saw. The most frequently expressed accusation
was that this was simply the drama of abnormality and
had nothing to say to normal readers and theatregoers.
An objection of more substance came from Gerhard
Gran who felt that a character of Hedda's complexity
could more effectively have been dealt with in a novel:

> Everything that should make this curious being intelligible to
> us, her development, her secret thoughts, her half-sensed
> misgivings and all that vast region of the human mind
> which lies between the conscious and unconscious – all this
> the dramatist can no more than indicate. For that reason, I
> think a novel about Hedda Gabler could be extremely
> interesting while the play leaves us with a sense of emptiness
> and betrayal. (Quoted from Meyer, p. 670)

To concentrate, as Gran does in his analysis, on an
individual character in all her mysterious impenetrability,
is a complete misunderstanding of Ibsen's dramatic
method. In this, as in his other mature plays, Ibsen is
fascinated by the dynamics of human relationships, viz.
what we do to each other, rather than with the
complexities of isolated individuals. What gives this play
its peculiar depth and resonance is the way he shows his
characters interacting within a specific and precise social
context. From the perspective of someone interested in
isolated individuals, *Hedda Gabler* might indeed be
interpreted as a drama of abnormality or at best a play
leaving one 'with a sense of emptiness and betrayal'. But
from a social and interactional perspective, it is a
strangely moving and poignantly dark comedy exploring
the life chances and expectations of men and women in
a highly competitive, male-dominated society.

One of the few perceptive responses to *Hedda Gabler*
from a contemporary writer came from Herman Bang.
In a lecture delivered in Kristiania in November 1891

Bang outlined the social basis for Hedda's dilemma:

> Most of Ibsen's plays had been about egotistical men and
> selfless women; but here was a play about an egotistical
> woman, and whereas a man's egotism may at least often
> cause him to accomplish much, a woman's merely drives
> her into isolation and self-adoration. Hedda has no source
> of richness in herself and must constantly seek it in others,
> so that her life becomes a pursuit of sensation and
> experiment; and her hatred of bearing a child is the
> ultimate expression of her egotism, the sickness that brings
> death. (Quoted from Meyer, p. 672)

In this, as in his other social plays, Ibsen's primary aim
was to show 'human beings, human moods and human
destinies, seen against a background of contemporary
social conditions and attitudes' (letter to Count Moritz
Prozor, 4 December 1890, *Oxford Ibsen*, vol. vii, p. 500).

## The geographical and stage environment

The action of *Hedda Gabler* takes place in 'Tesman's villa
in the fashionable quarter of town' ['West End' in the
Norwegian text]. Although Ibsen never specified which
city he had in mind as the setting for his play, it is
generally assumed he was thinking of Norway's capital,
which was then called, not Oslo, but Kristiania (prior to
1877 the official spelling was Christiania). All the
circumstantial evidence in the play points in this
direction. Tesman's house formally belonged to the
widow of a cabinet minister whom one would expect to
live in the capital. The west end of Kristiania where the
house was situated, i.e. in the area around Drammensvejen,
was the most expensive and fashionable part of town.
Furthermore, the kind of social life and entertaining
Hedda envisages would only have been feasible in
Kristiania: no other Norwegian city was large enough. It
also seems highly unlikely that any other Norwegian city
would have boasted an establishment quite like
Madamoiselle Danielle's parlour. On that score, the

Norwegian scholar, Halvdan Koht, in his introduction to
*Hedda Gabler* in the Centenary Edition of Ibsen's plays,
seems to think that even Kristiania during the 1890s
would have been an unlikely setting for such an
establishment (Henrik Ibsen, *Samlede verker, hundreårsutgave*,
vol xi, p. 282). Indeed Koht suggests that for this and
other reasons the play seemed foreign and un-Norwegian
to people during the 1890s. But perhaps one should treat
Koht's views with some scepticism. Kristiania in the
1890s was a lively seaport with a well-established red
light area near the harbour; it also boasted a flourishing
Bohemian subculture. On the evidence of the play itself,
and from what is known of historical and social
developments in late nineteenth-century Norway, *Hedda
Gabler* is based on the same acute and precise
observation of Norwegian society one finds in earlier
plays by Ibsen.

The social attitudes one finds expressed in the play
will be dealt with in the next section. But what were the
social conditions Ibsen might have observed during his
visit to Kristiania in 1885 and which are reflected in the
play itself? Probably the first and most obvious point to
note is that Kristiania, during the latter half of the
nineteenth century, was a town that grew almost visibly
day by day. Industrialisation had come late to Norway
and, consequently, the move from the countryside to the
towns only really began in the latter half of the
nineteenth century. In 1850 the population of the city
was 42,000: by 1900 it was 229,100. This type of growth
had a tremendous impact on the physical shape of the
town itself between the 1850s (when Ibsen had been a
student there) and the 1880s (when Ibsen paid only his
second visit to the city since the 1850s). Apart from the
new suburbs that were established, whole areas of
working-class slums were razed to the ground to make
way for prestige middle-class developments. For instance,
the slum quarters built on Ruseløkkbaken known as 'The
Robber States of Algiers and Tunis' were cleared in the
early 1880s to make way for the elegant flats known as

Victoria Terrasse, where Ibsen later came to live. New
working-class slums appeared further out from the city
centre, to the north and east, while more wealthy
members of the upper classes built their villas along
fashionable roads in the west end of town.

An important feature in the development of Kristiania
emerges from a description of the city written in the
early 1880s by a German visitor called Ludwig Passarge:

> Seventy years ago Christiania had hardly more than ten
> thousand inhabitants; but now one hundred and twenty
> thousand people live here, admittedly most of them in far-
> flung suburbs which, with their villas, gardens, harbours and
> factories, are very different from the familiar pattern of our
> old European cities.
>
> Mostly, people have built themselves detached houses
> along already existing roads. But speculators have also
> moved in, bought up large areas of land, and divided these
> up into regular plots which they have then sold off. In this
> way the suburbs of Grønland, Grünerløkken and Homansby
> were created. In general, however, there is a pleasing
> irregularity of lay-out, such as one finds it in hardly any
> other major city. The overall impresssion given is of a
> spacious, large and randomly structured spa town. [. . .]
>
> [By comparison with the castle grounds] there is an even
> greater variety of vegetation to be observed if one follows
> Drammensvej from south of the castle. [. . .] Here the
> wealthy citizens of Christiania have shown what can be
> achieved in the design and building of large villas when a
> hilly terrain stands obligingly at man's disposal and adds a
> distinct advantage in terms of planning. (Ludwig Passarge,
> *Drei Sommer in Norwegen. Reiseerinnerungen und Kulturstudien*,
> Leipzig, 1881, pp. 22 and 28)

What differentiated Kristiania from towns in central
Europe was its preponderance of detached houses with
their own gardens, in pleasingly landscaped settings. This
would certainly have struck Ibsen, coming back to
Kristiania from Germany after an absence of some thirty
years. It was therefore not fortuitous that he chose to

locate the action of *Hedda Gabler* in a villa. What was
surprising was locating this villa in the fashionable part
of town. This is where one might expect a general's
daughter to live, but for a young university professor, the
situation seems a little over-ambitious.

Turning now to the stage directions* for Act One,
they read as follows:

> A large drawing-room, handsomely and tastefully furnished;
> decorated in dark colours. In the rear wall is a broad open
> doorway, with curtains drawn back to either side. It leads to
> a smaller room, decorated in the same style as the drawing-
> room. In the right-hand wall of the drawing-room a folding
> door leads out to the hall. The opposite wall, on the left,
> contains french windows, also with curtains drawn back on
> either side. Through the glass we can see part of a veranda,
> and trees in autumn colours. Downstage stands an oval
> table, covered by a cloth, and surrounded by chairs.
> Downstage right, against the wall, is a broad stove tiled with
> dark porcelain; in front of it stands a high-backed armchair, a
> cushioned footrest and two footstools. Upstage right, in an
> alcove, is a corner sofa, with a small, round table. Downstage
> left, a little away from the wall, is another sofa. Upstage of
> the french windows, a piano. On either side of the open
> doorway in the rear wall stand what-nots holding ornaments
> of terracotta and majolica. Against the rear wall of the
> smaller room can be seen a sofa, a table, and a couple of
> chairs. Above this sofa hangs the portrait of a handsome, old
> man in general's uniform. Above the table, a lamp hangs
> from the ceiling with a shade of opalescent, milky glass. All
> round the drawing-room bunches of flowers stand in vases
> and glasses. More bunches lie on the tables. The floors of
> both rooms are covered with thick carpets. Morning light.
> The sun shines in through the french windows.

The most striking thing about this room, especially if one
compares it with some of Ibsen's other stage settings, is
the amount of elegant furnishing it contains. With its

---

* Contrary to normal practice, Ibsen describes his sets as viewed from the
auditorium.

different groupings of tables, chairs and sofas, this is obviously a room designed for social intercourse. We learn later the house has been furnished on borrowed money during the honeymoon of Tesman and Hedda by Aunt Juliana, aided and abetted by Judge Brack. What seems equally certain, however, is that Hedda, who intends playing the role of society hostess, has left very careful instructions as to how her house is to be furnished. Consequently, this drawing-room bears all the hallmarks of her aristocratic pretensions. In an average middle-class home, the drawing-room would not even be heated on a regular basis. The furniture would also be kept carefully preserved under loose covers. Hedda, of course, will have none of this, much to Auntie Juju's surprise. She intends living like a lady of quality and not like the wife of a bourgeois academic.

Another interesting feature about this stage setting is the upstage room adjoining the reception room. In a typical upper middle-class home of the period, this would have been the gentlemen's smoking room and, in an academic family, might have housed the study and library of the *pater familias*. In this play, however, the portrait of General Gabler in the room makes it quite apparent that this is Hedda's room. Another small but interesting feature is the fact that the thick carpeting from the reception room has been continued into this upstage room. Normally only the drawing-room was carpeted in this fashion. By continuing the carpeting into the additional room, Hedda has clearly indicated that she wants more than the usual drawing-room area for her social happenings and events.

The theme of elegance and spaciousness is continued into the outdoors part of the setting. Through the french windows, stage left, there is a view across a covered veranda towards trees turning an autumnal yellow. In its turn, this implies a reasonably large garden, the kind of garden in which Hedda can practise with her pistols without terrifying the neighbours. The draft confirms that this is indeed what Ibsen had in mind:

> The Tesmans' garden with a view over the fjord and the
> islands. Tall old lime trees on either side. Under a tree on
> the right, a garden bench with a table. In the middle, a
> fountain surrounding by flowering plants. The garden slopes
> down towards the back. (*Oxford Ibsen*, vol. vii, p. 292)

All of which makes Tesman's villa sound a very
expensive town property. Ibsen himself describes it in his
notes as 'a beautiful villa'.

A possible source of inspiration for this beautiful villa,
with its view towards the fjord, may have been the
property owned by Thomas Heftye, a wealthy banker
who was an acquaintance of Ibsen and a patron of the
arts. The house and its garden at no. 79 Drammensvej
have a number of features in common with those
described in Ibsen's stage directions both in the draft and
the final version of the play. (Today, Heftye's house is
the residence of the British Ambassador in Oslo.)
Although there can be no certainty that it was this house
alone that stimulated Ibsen's creative fantasy, its interior
and its grounds are sufficiently similar to those described
by Ibsen to give a very clear indication of the kind of
elegant life-style to which the Tesmans aspired.

Hedda, typically, takes such luxury for granted and
then treats it with disdain. In the play (as opposed to the
draft), she never actually sets foot in the garden, though
she shoots playfully at Brack as he walks through it. And
as for the house, she admits to Brack that she lied about
liking it. For her, it was something that enabled her to
engage Tesman in conversation in one of his more
tongue-tied moments. She simply pretended to like it.
Now that she actually lives in it, she dislikes the smell of
lavender bags and pomanders in all the rooms, but
accepts that it will at least provide her with an
acceptable framework for her socialising. Importantly
therefore one should realise that the stage setting
represents elegantly structured space rather than a home.

Only one corner of the room fulfils anything like a
homely function for Hedda. Significantly, she always
moves there when she feels most herself, namely in a

mood of genuine well-being or equally genuine rage. The area in question is downstage right by the stove with its grouping of high-backed armchair, footrest and two footstools. Symbolically perhaps Hedda feels drawn towards the stove, which, like her, has a smooth glazed exterior, concealing the naked flames, the constantly burning fire within.

The upstage room, with its central portrait of General Gabler, provides an obvious focus of attention. Seen through the curtained opening, it looks rather like a sanctuary in a church, viewed through an ornate screen. This is exactly how Hedda uses it. It is her sanctuary, containing the image of the God she worships and the altar of her past aspirations and ambitions, on which she will eventually sacrifice herself. Because of its visually dominant position, the room also provides a useful upstage entrance and exit at emotive points in the action.

The french windows to the garden serve two main functions during the action. Firstly, they seem to represent an opening out into a world of romantic spontaneity: they are significantly doors, not just windows. Hedda, sometimes in irritation at Tesman or his Auntie Juju, drums impatiently with her fingers against their glass panes. She would love to escape into the outside but dare not. At other times she looks out wistfully at a September landscape which seems only to echo the melancholy in her own soul. At such moments, Hedda can see no point in even trying to escape. She therefore chooses not to go out. Secondly, the french windows are also something of a threat. They are in fact a back way into the house, as well as being a possible exit. Significantly, Judge Brack, who is both a friend and a potential threat to Hedda, uses the french windows as a convenient back entrance into the house. The covered veranda outside the french windows serves no functional purpose but it does enhance the sense of affluence and status associated with the house. The folding door stage right that leads out into the hall is a neutral and formal entrance and exit, which is used by guests and Tesman.

(Significantly perhaps Tesman would not think of using the back way.) Brack uses this main entrance on formal and more sombre occasions.

The layout of the furniture is particularly interesting in this set. There is a lot of it, in distinct and separate groupings, clearly designed to facilitate different types of conversation and interaction. During the course of Act One, the furniture in the little room is not used at all. The room obviously interconnects with other parts of the house, and its main purpose in Act One is accordingly to provide effective upstage entries for Hedda and Tesman and a final threatening exit by Hedda. The corner sofa upstage right is not used, nor is Hedda's piano. On the other hand, Hedda does refer to the piano quite explicitly as her 'old piano' which 'doesn't really go with all this', i.e. the remaining furniture in the room. As a momento of her past, it would be better placed in her private sanctuary. By the beginning of Act Two, this is where it is moved.

The centre and downstage groupings of furniture have three distinct functions. The oval table centre is reserved in Act One for business and formal matters. Significantly Brack and Tesman discuss at the table the various loans and debts Tesman has incurred in setting up home in a sufficiently lavish way to please Hedda. It is also at that same formal table that Tesman learns of Eilert Loevborg's desire to compete for the chair in cultural history, the chair virtually promised in advance to Tesman. Without the prospect of a professor's salary, Tesman faces financial ruin: even he is jolted up out of his seat at that prospect.

The sofa downstage left is used freely by Tesman and Hedda for family and other intimate conversations. Clearly it is intended to be a place for relaxed and spontaneous interaction, although Hedda, who finds it difficult to be relaxed and spontaneous with anyone, forces her 'friend' Thea to sit there in order to interrogate her. The final group of furniture is Hedda's own private corner by the stove downstage right, with an

easy-chair, a footrest and two footstools. From a very
early point in the act, Hedda associates herself with this
area, moving there in some distress when Tesman tries
to rouse her enthusiasm for the slippers that Auntie Juju
has just brought him. Later in Act One, Hedda uses her
private corner as the ideal place in which to intensify her
interrogation of Thea. Forcibly placing Thea in her own
chair by the stove, Hedda pulls up one of the stools
close to the chair and literally puts the heat on her 'dear
friend'. Finally, at the end of the act, Hedda sits
pointedly in her chair while Brack is discussing sordid
matters such as money and work with Tesman. She
refuses to join them at the table. Another revealing touch
is the way she leans back lazily, and doubtless seductively
in her chair, to say goodbye to Brack. It is by the stove
then that we see Hedda most characteristically at home
in her own fantasy world. Only one other stage area
competes significantly for her attention, namely the
french windows. At several points in the play, and
already in Act One, she moves at moments of particular
stress between these two areas, from flame to light and
back again.

One further point can be made about the set for Act
One. Ibsen specifies that it contains a large number of
bouquets, obviously filling the room with colour and
perfume. Hedda dislikes them. She does not say why,
although in Act Two she does comment that the whole
house has a sort of 'odour of death. Like a bouquet the
day after a ball'. For her, then, flowers seem associated
with death or at least with the evanescence of pleasure.
The fact that there might be beauty and substance even
in evanescence is a thought that would never occur to
Hedda, such is her autumnal melancholy. (The autumnal
colours of the garden mirror her inner mood.)

The stage setting for Act Two includes a few small
but significant changes. Hedda's piano has been moved
into her sanctuary; in its place upstage left there is now
a writing desk, which is shown to be hers. Hedda stands
next to it, aiming one of her pistols, or rather one of her

father's pistols, out through the french windows. The
pistol case, containing the pair to the weapon she is
using, lies on the desk. Shortly afterwards, when Brack
has symbolically disarmed her, Hedda locks away both
pistols in the drawer of the writing desk, clearly
establishing it as a place where she can keep her secrets.

Another change in the furniture is the addition of a
small table by the sofa downstage left: later in the act, its
purpose as a drinks table becomes clear. Hedda uses it
as a means of placing temptation, in the shape of two
glasses of cold punch, quite literally under Loevborg's
nose. Finally, most of the flowers have been removed by
the beginning of Act Two, with the exception of Mrs
Elvsted's bouquet, now given a prominent place on the
table stage centre. The dominant visual position given to
the bouquet suggests that Mrs Elvsted, as Hedda's rival
for the affection of Eilert Loevborg, is beginning to play
something of a central role in Hedda's thoughts.

At the beginning of Act Two, Hedda moves from her
writing desk to the corner sofa on the opposite side of
the room. Brack has just joined her in the room and
seats himself on a convenient chair by the table stage
centre. From these two positions they flirt and spar with
each other in a cautious, even slightly formal manner.
Although Hedda leans back in the sofa as she begins to
enjoy the conversation, the fact that it takes place so far
upstage, and with some distance between Brack and
herself, indicates that it is not as intimate as it would be
in one of the downstage areas. For this kind of social
sparring, the formal corner sofa is ideally suited. It is the
only occasion in the play when it is used. After a while,
Tesman interrupts their conversation. When it resumes,
Hedda reveals far more of her real feelings and
frustrations to Brack. Significantly, she moves to her own
chair by the stove as she does so.

During the course of Act Two, Hedda gives
instructions to the maid for her sanctuary to be used as
a smoking room for the gentlemen. Perfectly aware that
this would be its normal function, Hedda is willing to see

it used as such as long as she controls when and for how
long. While Brack and Tesman smoke their cigarettes
and drink cold punch in what is effectively 'her' smoking
room, Hedda entertains Loevborg in the area of the
downstage sofa. Loevborg, like Hedda, gravitates at first
towards the stove; in him too there is a naked flame
smouldering beneath his reformed exterior. Hedda invites
him to pull up a chair by the sofa downstage left,
ostensibly to look at a photograph album with her, but
in fact to talk about their past and present relationship.
The invitation is expressed without words. Hedda sits in
the upstage corner of the sofa, which means that if
Loevborg does not wish his face to be seen by Brack
and Tesman, who are sitting in Hedda's sanctuary, he
must of necessity pull up a chair and sit with his back to
them. This is exactly what he does. Even after Thea's
entry, Hedda insists on keeping her position on the sofa,
pointedly placing herself *between* Loevborg and Thea.

Visually the scene is very effective, with Hedda ideally
placed to destroy the relationship between Thea and
Loevborg, knowing full well that Brack will be watching
every move they make from his upstage vantage point.
Deftly using the threat of Brack's watching eyes as the
means of stifling the merest hint of an emotional
outburst, Hedda coolly wrecks Loevborg's faith in Thea
and himself.

Hedda stage-manages this particular scene superbly. At
other points in the act, in fact on three different
occasions, she feels sufficiently irritated and threatened by
a chance remark to move towards the french windows,
as if longing to escape. At the end of the act, however,
she triumphs. So effective is her intervention in the cosy
relationship Loevborg has established with Thea that
Loevborg's iron resolve snaps and he agrees to take part
in Brack's bacchic feast. Inspired by the romantic image
of him returning from the feast with a crown of vine
leaves in his hair, Hedda triumphantly and almost
forcibly drags Thea off to afternoon tea. Significantly,
they exit through Hedda's private sanctuary.

At the beginning of Act Three the room is almost in darkness. The curtains are drawn across the french windows and across the entrance to Hedda's room. Hedda lies asleep on the sofa, Mrs Elvsted sits wrapped in a blanket on Hedda's chair. The stove door is open although the fire has almost burnt itself out. Throughout the act, fire symbolism plays a dominant role. One of the very first things Hedda does, after drawing open the curtains by the french windows, is to kneel down by the stove and start raking life back into the fire embers. One cannot imagine Hedda soiling her hands with any other household chore, but fire is her natural element and she associates herself freely with it. By the end of the act, the fire she has kindled comes to play a fateful role in the development of the action.

During the central section of the act Hedda listens first to Tesman's and then to Brack's account of Eilert's lapse into a state of drunken dissipation during the night. While he talks, Tesman sits on one of the stools warming himself at the stove. In a cautiously formal mood, Brack sits at the table stage centre. On both occasions, Hedda also sits at the table stage centre in a pose of studied unconcern.

After Brack's exit through the 'back door', the final showdown takes place between Thea, Loevborg and Hedda. All three characters remain standing during this highly charged scene. Loevborg enters, as one would expect, from the hall. Thea, on the other hand, enters through the curtains from Hedda's sanctuary. Her entrance from Hedda's room underlines visually just how firmly she is now caught in Hedda's trap. Hedda remains silent, in order to destroy the remaining vestiges of trust between Thea and Loevborg. After Thea's distraught exit, Hedda gives Loevborg, not his manuscript, but one of General Gabler's pistols so that he may at least die nobly and beautifully.

At the end of the act, Hedda is left alone on stage. Taking Loevborg's manuscript from her desk, she moves downstage to her chair by the stove and proceeds to

burn the manuscript page by page. As she does so, she makes it perfectly clear that she is in fact burning Loevborg and Thea's child. Seated in front of the open door of the stove, she gives in to the chaos of feeling inside her, as her façade cracks and her pent-up emotions break through in an act of savage destruction. Just as Loevborg's manuscript is consumed by flames inside the stove, she too is consumed by flames of emotion she can no longer control. She and the fire are one.

Act Four brings some significant changes in the use of stage space. At the beginning of the act, only the upper room, Hedda's sanctuary, is lit. Already, through this simple expedient, our attention is focused on this part of the stage. As the action progresses, it comes to play an increasingly dominant role. So far, Hedda has exercised a determining influence in the play on the way the stage space is structured and used. It was, for instance, she who decided where Thea would sit, where Loevborg would sit and when Brack and Tesman would be allowed to use her sanctuary as a smoking room. In Act Four, however, this pattern of control changes drastically. Instead of Hedda controlling the moves of the others, they now control what space will be left to her. The process begins with the unthinkable: Tesman and Thea take over her private sanctuary to begin piecing together Loevborg's manuscript notes. Then they vacate her private room to occupy Hedda's writing desk as the light is not good enough in the inner room. When Hedda moves to one of the chairs by the stove, Brack stands behind her and dominates her with his veiled threats. Even when Hedda leaves them all to take refuge in her private room, she is forbidden to play her piano by Tesman. She can also hear Tesman plotting to leave her alone every evening with Brack while he works on Loevborg's manuscript notes with Thea at Auntie Juju's house. Her personal space, indeed her whole life, are no longer under her control. Visually her defeat could not be more clearly indicated. In Acts One and Two she

had determined the pattern of moves in the play like a powerful grand master. Now she is reduced to a state of pitiful retreat into a sanctuary over which she no longer has ultimate control. In visual terms, Ibsen has prepared us for Hedda's response to her entrapment: a defiant act of suicide.

Rushing into Hedda's sanctuary to admonish her yet again, Tesman is thunderstruck by what he sees. He simply cannot begin to understand what is happening. Brack, on the other hand, seated in Hedda's chair by the stove, discovers just how dangerous it is to play with fire. The total incongruity of his response, 'But good God! People don't do such things!' indicates the depth of his shock and astonishment. Even Brack, for the first time in his life, is visibly seared by this explosive release of emotion in Hedda. For her part, Hedda is perfectly aware that in shooting herself she will regain her determining influence over the way the others move and interact in her domain. Not for nothing is she a general's daughter.

## The relationships  *Hedda · possession.*

### Hedda and Tesman

From the very opening of *Hedda Gabler*, one of the most notable features in the play is the sense of violent antagonism radiating from Hedda. In her very first scene on stage, when she enters to find Tesman's Auntie Juju paying an unsociably early call, the stage directions indicate the depth of her irritation in her pattern of movement. Throughout the scene, she is in constant motion, moving from an upstage position to the stove downstage right, from the stove to the table, and from the table to the french windows. It is as if she feels trapped by the environment and the people in it and longs to free herself from both. Even by the french windows, however, she finds Auntie Juju coming towards her to touch her, take her head into her hands and kiss it. Hedda has made her bed, as she later observes, and

finds that she has to lie on it.

When one looks at the dialogue to discover the specific events that provoke Hedda's antagonism, these seem in the first instance connected with the difference in social class between herself, on the one hand, and her husband and his Auntie Juju, on the other. Hedda, as a general's daughter, clearly sees herself as an aristocrat and shares a typical aristocratic belief in man's utter ruthlessness, a ruthlessness that can only be controlled by adhering to the strictest rules of political and social decorum. Hence her insistence on observing formal social proprieties. Auntie Juju, for instance, is firmly rebuked for not knowing the proper time to call, 'Good morning, dear Miss Tesman. What an early hour to call. So kind of you.'

Equally typical for her class is the admiration she feels for successful men who know all the rules so well that they can circumvent them with flair and intelligence without ever being trapped. Tesman, her husband, is so lacking in social graces that he has no idea what the rules are, let alone how to circumvent them. Hedda has only married him for his prospects, in the hope that, as his wife, she can at least act out the role of a society lady. But now that their honeymoon, quite literally, is over, she finds that his world, with its fundamentally different life-style and ideology, is going to make demands on her. This is something she had not bargained for.

Tesman's is the world of the thrifty, ambitious and hard-working bourgeoisie. Orphaned as a child, he was brought up by his kindly maiden aunts. Tesman has completely assimilated their values and their patterns of thought. He is used to a home filled with warmth and cosy sentimentality, a place that can act as a buffer against the harsher realities of life, which are never discussed or mentioned, if at all possible. His is not a ruthless world, but it is nevertheless quite effective at looking after its own interests. Tesman has been taught to be proud of his success and proud of his possessions.

That is why he is proud of Hedda. She is a prized possession and 'owning' her gives him reflected glory, as his aunt comments, 'And to think it's you who've won Hedda Gabler! The beautiful Hedda Gabler. Fancy! She was always so surrounded by admirers.' Hedda had of course knowingly allowed herself to be bought by Tesman: theirs was an almost purely commercial transaction. She needed his money and potential status and he wanted her as a possession. What Hedda had not foreseen was the fact that, having bought her, Tesman, as part of the transaction, would expect her to share his interests and values. This she flatly refuses to do.

For both of them this conflict is emblematically brought to a head in the mundane image of Tesman's slippers. In the scene already mentioned, Tesman virtually insists on Hedda showing an interest in his old bedroom slippers, lovingly embroidered by the invalid Auntie Rena. And the way he insists makes it evident that he expects her to show an interest in the domestic relationships he has enjoyed with his aunties, 'since she's one of the family now'. Viewed from Hedda's perspective, Tesman's slippers are an emblem of all she despises in his world: its stuffy sentimentality; its tame domesticity; its virtuous but immensely boring maiden aunts who sacrifice themselves for others; its tiresome vulgarity and lack of good tone and its equally tiresome lack of human depth and complexity. It was bad enough to hear Tesman talking about his slippers during their honeymoon; now she finds she is expected to show some enthusiasm for them in reality and, in so doing, to show some enthusiasm for everything they represent. This she refuses to do.

There is a kind of stubborn bravery in the way Tesman brings things to a head. For all his deference to Hedda as a superior social being, he does try to assert his 'masculine authority' and bend her to his will. But now he too finds that he has got more than he bargained for in his contract with Hedda. He may be

stubborn, but, when Hedda is provoked, she is positively reckless. What now happens in many ways foreshadows what is to happen in the remainder of the play. Hedda is confronted by a situation that she finds threatening and disturbing. Instinctively, she responds by hitting out with an almost feral lack of restraint. In this particular instance, the scale is small and the potential harm done is limited, but the pattern is nevertheless quite clear. Tesman has threatened her by insisting that she take an active interest in his world. Hedda responds to the threat by hitting out at a defenceless part of his world. She attacks his sweet, harmless and much loved Auntie Juju. Tesman had threatened her with an emblem from his world, namely his slippers. She now picks on another emblem from his world as the vehicle for her counter attack. She deliberately mocks Auntie Juju's hat, suggesting it is both old and socially vulgar (only something the maid would wear). In doing so, Hedda of course knowingly insults Auntie Juju and all that she represents, including the various social and family demands Auntie Juju would dearly love to make of Hedda. Hedda's attack is savagely effective. Poor Auntie is stung to the quick and pays dearly for her visit at an unsociably early hour. Tesman, with symbolic impotence, drops his beloved slippers to the floor, 'appalled'. Faced with that kind of recklessness, he is completely out of his depth. Significantly, all he can do now is cluck and fuss over Auntie Juju. He feels, and indeed Hedda wants him to feel, completely alienated from his wife.

With the help of her deliberate attack on Auntie Juju, Hedda has so far managed to retain control over the nature of her interaction with Tesman. Suddenly this changes. Tesman recovers his composure with surprising swiftness. Having done so, he deftly reasserts himself vis-à-vis Hedda by reminding her of the status she enjoys as one of his possessions. Admittedly her behaviour at times is a little wild, rather like an unruly spaniel, but she is still his cherished prize, 'But Auntie Juju, take a good look at Hedda before you go. Isn't she pretty and

charming?' And what is more, she is obviously blossoming under his regime, 'Yes, but have you noticed how strong and healthy she's looking? And how she's filled out since we went away?' Tesman here talks of Hedda as if she were a gun-dog who had been off her food for a while but is now doing remarkably well and filling out nicely. (And the gun-dog image is one Ibsen uses in his notes, 'His solicitude for her is the same as one gives to a thoroughbred horse or a valuable gun-dog'.) One can almost feel Hedda squirming as Tesman says this, but he is of course only reminding her, in the nicest possible way, of the factual situation. She belongs to him as a piece of property and, as the owner, he has the right to be proud of her. Fortunately for him, Tesman is not aware of the wider implications of his remark about Hedda filling out. But Auntie Juju is, and so is Hedda.

Hedda is pregnant, which provides another set of reasons for her antagonism towards Tesman. It is difficult enough to imagine Hedda and Tesman lying in bed together, let alone making love. (It probably happened the night they spent at Gossensass and met all those 'amusing people'. There is just a hint of this possibility when Hedda and Tesman comment on their honeymoon photographs to Loevborg.) But the thought of Hedda being pregnant and actually carrying George Tesman's child seems, and certainly to Hedda it seems, almost unbelievable. For her it is also an unendurable thought. At an everyday level, pregnancy would curtail her freedom and drastically reduce the various social options open to her. It would also make her more beholden to Tesman and his aunts. And after pregnancy would come motherhood with its demands and loss of personal freedom. This is a prospect Hedda dreads. It simply does not fit in with being a busy society hostess, who intends to ride her bay mare during the day and keep open house in the evening.

But there is another deeper reason for Hedda's rejection of the notion of pregnancy. Hedda is a woman

who has so far failed to come to terms with her own
femininity. Although she is a celebrated beauty who has
been fêted as a ballroom belle, hers is a cool, almost
asexual kind of beauty. Significantly, she is jealous of
other women whose relaxed and spontaneous femininity
fills her with envy. She would, for instance, love to burn
off Thea Elvsted's superb head of hair; her own hair is
described in the stage directions as 'of a handsome
auburn colour, but is not especially abundant'. One can
only speculate on the reasons for her difficulty in
accepting a clearly defined sexual role. But the title of
the play and the portrait of her father dominating the
upstage area provide important clues.

Hedda is still fundamentally her father's daughter. It is
from him that she derives her values and her view of the
world. When in trouble she turns to him for help, either
moving physically near his portrait in her sanctuary or
playing with the pistols that she has inherited from him.
There is of course an unmistakable phallic symbolism in
these pistols, and Hedda seems to use them whenever
she needs to show that she is a better man than any of
her would-be suitors. They also serve to underline the
fact that she is emotionally still dependent on her father
in a way that is inhibiting for the development of an
adult personality. In her marriage she seems to want to
continue essentially the same life she enjoyed as a
general's daughter without having the additional
responsibility of being a wife and a mother.

When one goes on to ask what life as a general's
daughter meant to Hedda, one gets the impression that
Hedda assimilated from her father a series of responses
appropriate for a young man in a man's world. Apart
from having learnt the obvious military skills of riding
and shooting, Hedda was taught to be ambitious,
ruthless, thrusting, always on her guard against scandal
and yet brave and even reckless in the face of danger.
Her upbringing, which would have been perfectly
appropriate for an upper-class young man in nineteenth-
century Norway, must have been for her, as a woman,

sexually, emotionally and socially confusing. Hedda, as
we see her in the play, is clearly still a victim of her
confusing upbringing, and a great deal of the chaos she
engenders in the world around her can be attributed to
it.

There are then class-based and deeply rooted
psychological reasons for Hedda's antagonism in the
opening scene of the play. She lives in a world that
appalls her with its sordidness and threatens her with its
emotional demands. Having sold herself as an object, to
become a beautiful doll wife in a male-dominated
society, Hedda finds there is no obvious outlet for her
energy and creativity. Confronted by this situation, she
creates a fantasy world of her own where people can be
manipulated and moved around like pieces in a game of
chess. Tesman and his Auntie Juju are, in this fantasy,
disposable pawns (the Norwegian word for pawns,
namely *bønder* or peasants, would in fact be more
appropriate). When, in reality, they refuse to play the
role of disposable peasants and instead turn round and
start making demands on Hedda, she reacts, one is
tempted to say, overreacts quite violently. Life, real life,
is not quite the game of chess she bargained for.

## Hedda and Brack

Another person who plays an important role in Hedda's
fantasy world is Judge Brack. For him too Hedda has
mapped out a certain pattern of moves and responses in
her game of human chess. Brack is like a nimble rook,
with whom she can castle, sharing certain formal
intimacies as she does so, before she sends him out on
hunting expeditions in foreign territory. To begin with,
Brack seems inclined to accept this role, but gradually he
too starts making demands on Hedda that threaten her
emotional equilibrium.

In contrast to Tesman, there is nothing mean and
vulgar about Brack. He is a man of the world, a man
whose profession it is to know all the rules by heart and,

of course, how to break them. Consider, for instance, the
way he stage-manages his unsociably early call by
comparison with Auntie Juju's unthinking *faux pas*. As he
enters the room, bowing with his hat in his hand, the
very first thing he says is, 'May one presume to call so
early?' To which there is only one possible answer, as he
is well aware. Brack is a man who knows his way
around, which is what makes him attractive to Hedda.
At the same time, he is far more dangerous than she at
first realises. Those very qualities that make him
attractive to her in fact guarantee that in the end he will
not be content to be her playmate.

It is not until Act Three that Brack begins to show his
claws, but when he does so, Hedda is left in no illusions
about his aims and intentions:

> **Hedda** (*looks at him and smiles*)   I see. You want to be the
> cock of the walk.
> **Brack** (*nods slowly and lowers his voice*)   Yes, that is my aim.
> And I shall fight for it with – every weapon at my disposal.
> **Hedda** (*as her smile fades*)   You're a dangerous man, aren't
> you? When you really want something.
> **Brack**   You think so?
> **Hedda**   Yes, I'm beginning to think so. I'm deeply
> thankful you haven't any kind of hold over me.
> **Brack** (*laughs equivocally*)   Well, well, Mrs Hedda – perhaps
> you're right. If I had, who knows what I might not think
> up?

In the previous act, Brack had been content to play
Hedda's game of sexual innuendo and flirtation. He had
hinted, however, that what he was hoping to establish
with her was a triangular relationship. The triangle he
envisaged was: boring husband, frustrated wife, dynamic
lover. Hedda had responded rather ambiguously. She
had likened her life to a tiresome railway journey,
although confessing she was too much of a coward to
jump out of the compartment. She was afraid of showing
her legs. She was not therefore willing to jump down onto
the platform to meet Brack on his terms; but he was

welcome to join her in the compartment, on her terms.

Brack had clearly anticipated from her the kind of reciprocity that might reasonably be expected from an unhappily married woman of his aristocratic class. In this respect, his expectations are identical to those of the cynical rake figure, Dorimant, in Sir George Etherege's Restoration comedy, *The Man of Mode* (1676). Lining up a future conquest, Dorimant comments, 'I have known women make a difficulty of losing a maidenhead who have afterwards made none of making a cuckold.' Like Dorimant, Brack assumed that Hedda would find little difficulty in cuckolding her husband, having carefully preserved her virginity until safely married. So far, he has played his role with impeccable good manners. Not intending to marry Hedda, he was content to escort her to balls and parties without pressing any claims on her. But now that she is safely married, he feels the rules of the game have changed. What he wants from Hedda, as he looks at her through his monocle and allows his fantasy free rein, is some adult fun. In a genuinely Epicurean fashion, he is convinced that what is pleasurable is good and what is not is bad. Unfortunately, Hedda does not seem to share his view. Perhaps she is just teasing him, perhaps she wants to be threatened, perhaps her tastes are more advanced than he thought. Brack tests the temperature of the water with a blatantly sexual threat, 'who knows what I might not think up?' However, Hedda is clearly not in the mood for advanced sexual games just yet, so Brack reverts to a more oblique suggestiveness in his parting shots, 'I've nothing against back doors. They can be quite intriguing – sometimes'. Hedda clearly understands the inference and reminds Brack of her earlier pot-shot at him out of the back door. To which he responds teasingly, 'Oh, people don't shoot tame cocks.' As he exits laughing, one can easily imagine the kind of 'sporting' evenings his fertile mind is planning. And so can Hedda.

From Hedda's point of view, Brack is yet another disappointment. She had envisaged him playing a vital

but controlled function in her innocent fantasy game. Now she suddenly finds that instead he expects her to play a compliant role in a very different game of his own devising. And what he has in mind is no game of chess. What she wants from Brack is companionship, gossip, erotic flirtation, but at a safe distance, a kind of pre-adult sexual reciprocity. Hedda simply cannot cope with adult emotions, adult sexuality, and adult responsibility. She wants Brack to be one of her emotional playmates, but importantly a playmate with enough self-control to know when to stop. Brack had dropped some hints earlier about the kind of triangular relationship he wanted to establish with her and Tesman, but at that point Hedda had still felt that she could control the nature of their relationship. In this scene in Act Three she realises for the first time that Brack is simply not willing to play the game according to her rules. As she grasps that Brack fully intends to reduce her to the status of a sexual object he can exploit, the smile slowly fades from her face. 'You're a dangerous man, aren't you? When you really want something.' This is the voice of adult recognition. Hedda is no longer playing childish games with Brack. When Brack leaves her at the end of this encounter, Hedda knows precisely the kind of role she would be expected to fill in one of his scenarios. She would be used and abused by a smooth-talking, but arrogant and ruthless sexual predator. That prospect fills her with revulsion. She would rather die than face that.

These are the two states of mind confronting each other in this scene. And they are two such disparate responses that there is hardly any meaningful contact between them. Although ostensibly they talk the same oblique language, their motives for using subtextual innuendo are radically different. Because their sensibilities are poles apart, Brack completely misinterprets Hedda's intentions, while Hedda for her part begins for the first time to see Brack for what he is. And what she sees, she does not like. For Hedda, this recognition is yet another

savage blow to the fantasy world she has constructed. Brack's misunderstanding, on the other hand, is more comic than serious. Although one should not underestimate the seriousness of his threat to Hedda, his playfulness suggests a fundamentally mistaken assumption on his part, namely that by sharing his joke, Hedda also shares his Epicurean view of the world.

As in so many other scenes in the play, there is a strange and disturbing mixture here of the comic and the serious. The audience is invited to respond with laughter at Brack's sexual innuendoes and at his misunderstanding of Hedda's intentions. But even as one laughs, one notices the smile fading from Hedda's face. One's laughter becomes uneasy, almost embarrassed. This same pattern is repeated throughout the play. An incongruous response, a complete misunderstanding produces laughter, but elsewhere on stage the reality and validity of a particular character's pain or suffering throws one's laughter into question.

### Hedda and Loevborg

Brack sees only the brittle superficial side of Hedda's personality, which is all he wants to see. Tesman regards Hedda with a mixture of pride and concern, as if she were a highly-strung thoroughbred that had cost him a small fortune. Thea Elvsted regards Hedda with a mixture of awe and fear; she has been frightened of Hedda since her school days when Hedda threatened to burn her hair off. Auntie Juju gives Hedda her blessing, 'for George's sake'. The only character in the play who even begins to understand the hidden depths in Hedda's personality is Eilert Loevborg. The scene between them in Act Two, as Ibsen himself observed in his preliminary notes, marks the turning point in the play.

Eilert was an aristocrat of the spirit for whom Hedda had felt an immediate affinity. She was brave enough to invite him home because he excited her in a way no one else ever had. He was a man who seemingly dared to

live out his fantasies and deepest longings. It was that that
made him so attractive to Hedda. Terrified of scandal,
terrified of being rejected (which may well be connected
with the lack of a mother figure in her life), Hedda was
always afraid of her hidden thoughts, ashamed of the
urges and desires she felt within her. When Eilert visited
her at home and talked to her about his secret life, right
under the very nose of General Gabler, Hedda lived a life
of erotic fulfilment, albeit vicariously. No wonder Eilert
became a fantasy hero for her.

For Eilert, as he himself says, Hedda became
something of a confessor. He needed to talk to her
about his various excesses because his behaviour was still
conditioned by feelings of guilt. In Hedda's eyes he was
a brave iconoclast who dared to live freely in defiance of
the world. In reality, he was a sensitive but somewhat
unstable personality who found himself driven to drink
and other excesses because he was unable to cope with
the world of everyday experience. His guilt-ridden
attempts at escape were anything but the behaviour of a
free man. Hedda at least offered him the opportunity to
confess all his sins.

There was a complementary quality in their
relationship at this stage, with each one fulfilling the
fantasy needs of the other. As Hedda expresses it, they
had achieved a beautiful comradeship in their life
together, 'there was something beautiful and fascinating –
and brave – about the way we told each other
everything. That secret friendship no one else knew
about.' Theirs was a glorious fiction that gave each of
them support and encouragement. In the end, it
disintegrated. And it did so at the very moment when
Eilert threatened, as Hedda says, to turn their game into
reality. Reality, with its pain, complexity and confusion,
was something Hedda could not cope with.

When Eilert made a pass at her, Hedda drove him
out of the house with her father's pistol. Subsequently,
Eilert, as Hedda correctly observes, 'found consolation
with the Elvsteds'. Thea Elvsted had at least given him

the kind of warmth and spontaneity of which Hedda had in the end proved incapable. They too had established a complementary relationship, although based on very different premises from the one between Eilert and Hedda. This time the shared fantasy was that of the domestic idyll. At last, Eilert found himself a woman who was willing to wash him free from guilt. In offering him her vision of uncomplicated warmth and domesticity, Thea helped Eilert to give up his old ways and to conform to a more respectable pattern of bourgeois living. The fact that she did this as a woman already married, albeit unhappily married, to a county sheriff, was proof of her commitment. Although in many ways Thea was too 'stupid', as Eilert puts it, ever to understand her hero in all his complexity, he nevertheless gladly accepted what she offered him, namely her loyalty, her faith and her commitment. In return, he gave her gratitude, respect and a far more genuine comradeship than he ever achieved with Hedda. Theirs too, however, was a relationship that could only thrive at some remove from reality. A reformed alcoholic enjoying an intimate 'friendship' with an unhappily married woman in her husband's own house, are not exactly the best ingredients for a domestic idyll. Not surprisingly, as soon as Eilert returns to town, the idyll is threatened.

Hedda's passing reference to Eilert finding consolation with the Elvsteds is brief but revealing. As always she hides her real feelings behind an oblique or ironic comment. But the fact that she makes the comment at all is indicative of the resentment and jealousy she feels towards Thea. Thea Elvsted, the silly goose whom she used to tease during their school days, has actually had the courage to commit herself to Eilert. She has joyfully shared ideas and experiences with him, and is now even willing to face scandal for his sake. (Thea has decided to leave her husband and commit herself totally to Eilert.) Thea has succeeded in turning Eilert into a reformed man. Her commitment has given her power over Eilert,

the kind of power Hedda once had, without realising it.
When Eilert assures her that she once did
have power over him, she savours the notion
thoughtfully, ominously, 'Power? You think I had some
power over you?' Reciprocity is threatening and
dangerous, but it gives one power over another. Hedda
finds the idea exciting, attractive and terrifying.

At the very end of her brief scene with Eilert in Act
Two, Hedda fumbles towards a new reciprocity with
him. She is determined to regain the power over him
she once enjoyed. Quietly and without daring to look
him in the eyes, she comes as close to declaring her real
feelings as she is ever likely to, 'But let me tell you
something. Something you don't know . . . My failure to
shoot you wasn't my worst act of cowardice that
evening.' So unexpected and stunning is this confession
of her real feelings for him that even Eilert takes some
time to assimilate what she is actually saying here.
However obliquely, Hedda confesses here that her
cowardice, as she calls it, the whole legacy of sexual and
social inhibitions with which she grew up, prevented her
from reaching out and grasping what Eilert offered her:
the reality of authentically shared experience, freely given
and freely enjoyed by two equals. Long years of
repressed and confused emotions held her back at the
crucial moment. She too wanted life and love, but she
was too frightened and too confused to respond openly
and freely to Eilert. A whole world of longing and
frustration opens up between the lines as Eilert looks at
her for a moment and gradually realises what she has
just said, 'Now I see what was behind those questions.
Yes! It wasn't knowledge you wanted! It was life!' Even
now, years after the event, Hedda's act of confession
causes her enormous emotional turmoil. And at once she
retracts it, rapidly denying what she has just said, 'Take
care! Don't you delude yourself!' Hedda still cannot
cope with reality. Genuine reciprocity would leave her
too vulnerable. In making and then retracting her
confession, however, she places both Loevborg and

herself in an untenable position. Whatever they do or do
not do after this is bound to be painful, confusing, and
destructive. Hedda has successfully placed them both in a
double bind. If they accept the status quo, then they do
so in the full knowledge of its pointless triviality by
comparison with what might have been. This would
effectively destroy the fantasy worlds within which they
have both lived. If they attempt to change the status
quo, it would be on the fragile basis of feelings whose
validity has just been denied in a deliberate act of bad
faith. Not to act (which is, as always, a form of action)
or to act are both impossible choices. Hedda's way out
of this dilemma is to retreat into yet another world of
fantasy. So far, her fantasies have been relatively
innocent and protective: from now on they become
aggressive and destructive. This scene marks the decisive
turning point.

*Conclusion*

There is energy and idealism in Hedda. As Ibsen said in
his notes, 'With Hedda, there is poetry in her deep
down.' But there is no outlet for it in the kind of society
in which she lives. All through her life, she has been
consistently taught to suppress and deny her real feelings.
Her deepest longing, as Eilert rightly suspected, was for
a life in which there could be authenticity, truth and
beauty: a life in which there could be genuine
intellectual, emotional and sexual reciprocity without
subterfuge and shame. Such a life was denied her by the
repressive values of her upbringing and her social
environment. Confused and alienated by the world of
reality, Hedda retreats into a fantasy world of her own,
in which she can express her longings obliquely, at one
remove from reality. During the course of the play,
however, every single fantasy image she creates is
destroyed. To begin with, her relatively innocent
fantasies are shattered one by one. Tesman's dubious

career prospects and her looming motherhood mean that she will not after all be able to act out the role of a carefree society hostess. Later her more aggressively destructive fantasies produce, not a world of poetic beauty, as she hoped, but grotesquely and comically distorted images of her intentions. Eilert disgraces himself in a drunken orgy when he should return to her with vine leaves in his hair. He then lets her down yet again by failing to die beautifully in a gesture of aristocratic contempt for the world and instead shoots himself accidentally in the genitals while arguing in a brothel. As she herself says, 'Oh, why does everything I touch become mean and ludicrous? It's like a curse!'

The real problem is that her fantasy world, which initially seemed to offer a blessed relief from the pain and frustration of everyday experience, inevitably produces its own pain and confusion. Initially she resorted to fantasy as a means of preserving her 'real', poetic, and idealistic self. Eventually, however, she loses her real self totally in the spiralling vortex of a fantasy world that has its own cruel laws. Trapped in that vortex, she finds herself in the end acting out the role of a child murderer as she destroys Eilert's manuscript, the spiritual child that he and Thea created together. Hedda's suppressed thirst for life initially drove her to defend herself with fantasy strategems: but in the end, these bring her to the point where she is no longer a life-enhancing idealist but a destructive killer.

At the close of the play, all that is left to Hedda as the sum total of her 'reality' are a number of intolerable images. The first is of Thea Elvsted establishing a new domestic idyll, only this time with Hedda's husband, George Tesman. Hedda's destruction of Eilert's manuscript has, if anything, enhanced Thea's standing as Eilert's spiritual companion. She has lovingly kept the notes of Eilert's destroyed masterpiece and can now play a crucial role in helping Tesman to piece them together. The second image is of Judge Brack confidently looking

forward to having his pleasure with her now that he can effectively blackmail her over the circumstances of Eilert's death. The third image is of the child growing in her womb, the child that will eventually imprison her with its as yet unknown demands.

Rather than face up to the threat of these various images, Hedda chooses to live out the last of her fantasy scenarios herself. She decides to become her own tragic heroine, dying nobly and beautifully, and with the kind of gesture of aristocratic contempt that she had expected from Eilert. Even now, however, success ultimately eludes her. There is something too spitefully irresponsible, too immature in her suicide to provoke the necessary mixture of pity and fear that is appropriate for a tragic heroine. Consequently, there is almost more comedy than tragedy in her going. The suddenness of her suicide produces a laughably absurd response from both Tesman and Brack:

> **Tesman** (*screams to* **Brack**)   She's shot herself! Shot herself in the head! Fancy that!
> **Brack** (*half paralysed in the armchair*)   But, good God! People don't do such things!

The incongruous nature of the deed robs it of any tragic dignity. Yet again, Hedda has behaved like an irresponsible child, thrusting from her the burden of living in an adult world and, in so doing, killing the young life growing within her.

Although Hedda fails to convince in her chosen role of tragic heroine, there is nevertheless something deeply disturbing in her fate. Hedda is intelligent and sensitive, perhaps even gifted, and yet she is so emotionally stunted by her upbringing, so cowed by the repressive values of her social environment that she cannot relate spontaneously and openly to any of the people around her. In emotional terms, this is completely disabling. Unable to relate to others, Hedda can achieve no satisfactory vision of what she herself is or even might

become.* All that is left her in the resulting emotional
vacuum in which she lives is the assumption of untenable
fantasy roles that are ultimately self-destructive in nature.

Hedda's suicide raises profound questions about the
nature of the society in which she lived. As a male-
dominated society, it offered no outlet for the energy and
creativity of a woman like Hedda. As a sexually and
emotionally repressed society, it fostered the growth of
neurosis and hysteria. As an acquisitive and materialistic
society, it tended to reduce male–female relationships to
the level of commercial transactions. The value of a
woman was determined exclusively by what a man was
willing to pay for her. Underneath the laughter in this
tragicomedy, Ibsen made crystal clear the price to be
paid, in terms of human misery and suffering, for living
in Hedda's repressed, middle-class world. *Hedda Gabler*
amounted to a crushing indictment of contemporary
European society and its acquisitive, competitive values.
Through the use of laughter and incongruity, the play
spoke to the mind as well as the heart. It was
deliberately written as a play that would challenge
audiences to examine the value structures underpinning
their world.

As always, Ibsen preferred to ask, not to answer. But
by underlining the precise social factors contributing to
Hedda's distressing psychological state, Ibsen invited his
audience to see that what happened to Hedda was not
the result of some ineluctable tragic fate but the result of
social process. In its turn, social process was not merely
a fortuitous collection of things that happen, but an
accumulation of deeds done by agents. Hedda's
behaviour can therefore be understood as a perfectly
intelligible response to deeds (and agents) that in various
ways have undermined and threatened her emotional

---

* As the psychiatrist R. D. Laing noted in his book, *Self and Others*
(Penguin Books, 1971, pp. 82 and 86), 'All "identities" require an other:
some other in and through a relationship with whom self-identity is
actualized [. . .] Every relationship implies a definition of self by other and
other by self.'

integrity and security.

For all the provocative dark comedy in *Hedda Gabler*, the play is ultimately constructive in intent. As in his other major plays, *Hedda Gabler* requires the active participation of an audience to complete the interpretation. At the end of the play Ibsen challenges the audience to think creatively and to envisage a society and a pattern of relationships in which a woman like Hedda need feel neither suppressed nor oppressed. His aim was to confront his audiences with a series of human destinies and dilemmas, seen in their precise social context, and then to challenge his audiences to arrive at their own solutions to the dilemmas shown. As early as 1875, Ibsen had clearly outlined his artistic approach in his poem *A Rhyming Letter*:

> Do not ask me, friend, to solve the riddle;
> I prefer to ask, it is not my task to answer.

This was a vision to which he remained faithful throughout his creative life. Accordingly, in *Hedda Gabler* he articulated a raft of difficult questions but was careful to avoid giving answers.

In most of Ibsen's plays we are confronted by images of failure and of stunted human potential in society as it at present exists. We are then challenged to think and feel our way intuitively toward our own alternatives to the various destructive patterns of interaction we have seen. This challenge provides the positive groundswell underneath even the darkest of Ibsen's plays. The record of failure is no more than a surface image, but the provocative manner in which failure is shown is Ibsen's declaration of faith in our ability to share with him a hidden, positive vision of human potential. Sometimes the provocation is emotive, as in *Ghosts*; elsewhere, as in *Hedda Gabler*, it is ironic and sardonic. But Ibsen's provocative vision is as fresh today as when he wrote for those who have learnt to read between the lines and see beyond the surface imagery to the hidden poetry underneath. Ibsen himself summed up the challenge he

gives to his readers and his audiences in the original epic version of his play *Brand*. It seems entirely appropriate therefore to conclude this discussion by giving Ibsen himself the last word.

> For my song I have tuned my instrument low,
> But undertones give resonance to the music.
> Hence there is a poem hidden in the poem,
> And whoever understands *that* will understand my song.

## *Hedda Gabler* in context

By the time he wrote *Hedda Gabler*, Ibsen had already established for himself a firm reputation as one of Europe's leading contemporary dramatists. In the early years of his career as a playwright, Ibsen had initially used conventional approaches to character and plot to explore largely national romantic themes. None of these early plays from the 1850s were of any real artistic merit, but images and themes from them recur in Ibsen's later work. For instance, in *Lady Inger of Østraat* (1855), Ibsen attempted to explore the complex and anguished state of mind of the main character in a way that foreshadows a play like *Hedda Gabler*. A theme that also recurs in *Hedda Gabler* is first explored in *The Warrior's Barrow* (1854), namely the clash between powerfully conflicting emotions in the main character.

Ibsen broke with this approach to playwriting when he left Norway in 1864 to begin a period of voluntary exile that was to last almost thirty years. His initial attempts to articulate a distinctive and pioneering voice as a mature playwright were marked by a joyful embrace of verse drama as a vehicle to explore a number of important existential issues. In *Brand* (1866) he probed the clash between human will-power and the inhibiting effect of the formative experiences that have shaped every personality. In *Peer Gynt* (1867), he explored the nature of selfhood and, in particular, the paradox (first articulated by Christ) that to be oneself is to lose one's

self. A final philosophical work, *Emperor and Gaililean*
(1873; written in prose and less vivacious and less easy to
assimilate), explored another set of issues that fascinated
Ibsen throughout his career, namely the clash of pagan
and Christian values. The Emperor, Julian the Apostate,
makes a hopeless attempt to reconcile these two
conflicting belief structures, but in the end finds himself
destroyed by the determining forces of historical
inevitability. Some of the ideas and images from this
play recur in *Hedda Gabler*. Hedda, like Julian, longs for
the pagan beauty of Dionysus and the ecstasy
experienced by his devotees. In reality, however, her
emotional longing for pagan spontaneity and ecstasy is
strangled by the oppressive values of the moralistic and
pietistic culture that predominated in Norway at the
time.

By the late 1870s, Ibsen had embarked on the third
and final phase of his career as a playwright. Inspired by
the progressive ideas of the Danish cultural historian,
Georg Brandes, Ibsen began a series of plays in which
he subjected contemporary issues and problems to
debate. The series began with *The Pillars of Society* (1877),
in which he explored the human consequences of early
capitalism in a small Norwegian town. But it was *A Doll's
House* (1879) that made him famous and *Ghosts* (1881)
that made him notorious. In both plays Ibsen presented
a withering critique of current patriarchal marriages.
He shows his women characters as victims of a society
that gives them no property rights in marriage, no legal
rights within the family and no democratic rights within
society. Ibsen denied that he was a feminist, but his
precise delineation of women's exploitation in marriages
at the time shocked and disturbed his contemporaries. *A
Doll's House* unleashed the debate. At the end of this
play, Nora quits her doll's house marriage, in which she
is just a pretty possession belonging to a patronising
husband, to discover who she is. In so doing, she leaves
both her husband and her children to face a life of
social exclusion and economic hardship. Even today, few

women are prepared to leave their children on the break-up of a marriage, which perhaps explains why Ibsen's play still seems such a challenging exploration of married life.

In *Ghosts*, Ibsen shows what happens when a wife who has left her husband is forced by social pressure to return. The result for both parties is a life of endless torment. Captain Alving turns to drink and serial adultery. Mrs Alving becomes judgemental and embittered. When Alving eventually makes his wife's chambermaid pregnant, Mrs Alving uses the threat of scandal to force her husband to hand over control of the estate. This wasteland of ruined lives and expectations is brought to a final and dreadful conclusion after Alving's death. Osvald, the Alvings' son, is struck down by the sins of his father. He has not only inherited his father's eye for a pretty girl (he attempts to seduce the maid Regine, unaware that she is his half-sister), he may also have inherited syphilis from his father. As Osvald lapses into a demented state at the end of the play, Mrs Alving is faced by the dreadful decision of whether or not to kill him as an act of mercy (as he has requested). The audience, for its part, is faced by a terrifying image of what life is really like behind the polite exterior of bourgeois society. Ibsen's readers and audiences were outraged. For years, the play could not be performed in any European theatre and irate customers returned unopened copies of the play to booksellers. With *Ghosts*, Ibsen had clearly touched a very raw nerve.

In the ten years that elapsed between *Ghosts* and *Hedda Gabler*, Ibsen went on to write some of his most subtle plays in which he probed complex patterns of interaction between the main characters. Plays like *The Wild Duck* (1884) and *Rosmersholm* (1886) baffled his contemporaries. The same was to be true of *Hedda Gabler*. Audiences at that time were not accustomed to seeing plays that were full of subtle characterisation, dialogue based on subtextual references and images, and complex plot structures that left issues unresolved. Throughout the

nineteenth century, plays in Europe had been simple to
follow and to understand. Even plays that ventured into
the area of social concern, like *La Dame aux Camélias* by
Dumas *fils*, had a clear structure and characters whose
behaviour followed predictable patterns of response.
Ibsen changed all that. He wrote plays that eschewed the
neat endings of the well-made play (as written by Scribe,
Sardou and Dumas *fils*) and the trivial banalities of the
English stage. His open endings, which left questions
hanging in the air, irritated middle-class critics and
theatre-goers who did not wish to be challenged in the
theatre. His exploration of complex psychological states
bewildered them. His frank exploration of social issues,
and in particular his blunt depiction of the tawdry secrets
of bourgeois family life, outraged them. But his sensitive
understanding of women's emotional and physical needs,
and his depiction of their exploitation in contemporary
marriages, won him many friends and admirers in
progressive circles throughout Europe. In England he
had outspoken champions in William Archer, Edmund
Gosse and George Bernard Shaw. For them he became
an icon of modern thinking. Their untiring support for
his work eventually helped Ibsen's plays to find their
rightful place in the repertoire of the English stage.

The Swedish playwright, August Strindberg, was
Ibsen's main rival within the sphere of contemporary
Scandinavian drama. The two writers pursued radically
different approaches in their plays. Ibsen, deeply
committed to the analysis of social and personal issues,
exploited naturalist and symbolist techniques to show the
way human beings create meaning or absurdity for each
other in the way they respond to each other's needs.
Strindberg used techniques that foreshadow expressionist
theatre, in order to articulate his vision of life's ultimate
absurdity. For Strindberg, it is only in the act of
playwriting and performance that absurdity can be
transcended. These two great Scandinavian playwrights
were life-long adversaries who had, at best, a grudging
admiration and, at worst, a hostile dislike of the work of

the other.

Ibsen's influence was enormous. Chekhov openly acknowledged his debt to Ibsen and even chose to name his play *The Seagull* as a deliberate echo of the title Ibsen had used for his play, *The Wild Duck*. Freud derived many of his key insights from Ibsen's work. Freud's personal collection of books includes heavily annotated editions of Ibsen's plays. Some of the concepts Freud elaborated in his work, for instance the notion of phallic symbols, are clearly stated and exploited in Ibsen's work. General Gabler's pistols are an obvious example; another is the tower in *The Master Builder* which Solness longs to climb but, in his impotence, cannot.

Ibsen's work has continued to provide a fertile source of inspiration for playwrights throughout the twentieth century. Dramatists who wish to explore social issues inevitably find themselves drawn to Ibsen. Arthur Miller is arguably the most distinguished disciple of Ibsen and, in particular, his play *All My Sons* is modelled closely on Ibsen's example. David Hare and Edward Bond are writers whose social plays also owe much to Ibsen's pioneering approach to character drawing and dialogue. However, even a writer like Harold Pinter, who is fascinated by the subtextual complexities of human discourse, finds himself using a similar approach to that of Ibsen in *Hedda Gabler*. Pinter, like Ibsen, exploits comic effects to reinforce the seriousness of the issues at stake. Ibsen is now justly seen as one of the great playwrights of his age. And, like all great playwrights, his work has inspired writers who have followed his example and has lent itself to a rich series of reinterpretations on the modern stage.

### *Hedda Gabler* on stage

The initial productions of *Hedda Gabler* took place in Germany and Scandinavia during January and February 1891. For differing reasons, they were all failures. Ibsen himself attended the world première of the play at the

Residenztheater in Munich on 31 January 1891. He
was appalled at the declamatory style of the actors,
which was at odds with the comic style of the
dialogue.* The great Danish naturalist director,
William Bloch, fared little better in his production of the
play at Copenhagen's Theatre Royal in February 1891.
His approach, with the veteran actress Betty Hennings in
the title role, lacked colour and vigour. The first
successful production of the play occurred in the unlikely
setting of the Vaudeville Theatre in London in April
1891. Generally, Ibsen's plays were heartily disliked by
London's stuffy, middle-class theatregoers and critics. The
last thing desired by audiences in Victorian London was
to have their prejudices challenged and their materialistic
values subjected to the kind of withering critique at
which Ibsen excelled. The critic Clement Scott was the
leading spokesman for this compact majority of middle-
class theatregoers. However, even he, much to his
surprise, found himself enthralled by the performance of
the American actress Elizabeth Robins as Hedda Gabler
in the Vaudeville Theatre production. In his review of
the production for the *Illustrated London News* of 25 April
1891, Scott wrote:

> Miss Elizabeth Robins approached her task with artistic
> glee, and crowned it with undoubted success. The lovers of
> sustained art should not miss it, even if the play itself shocks
> them. The character grew under the influence of the actress.
> Her face was a study. No one could move their eyes from
> her. [. . .] She has made vice attractive by her art. [. . .]
> She has made a heroine out of a sublimated sinner. She has
> fascinated us with a savage. (Quoted from Michael Egan
> (ed.), *Ibsen: The Critical Heritage*, p. 227)

Elizabeth Robins's approach to the role was based upon
a close psychological study of Hedda's character and
responses. The primary quality that she brought out in

* For more detailed descriptions of these productions see Frederick J.
Marker and Lise-Lone Marker, *Ibsen's Lively Art: A Performance Study of the
Major Plays*, pp. 163–7.

performance was the 'demonic' side to Hedda's personality. It was this that fascinated Miss Robins's admirers and even those who were normally repelled by Ibsen's work. Her painstaking analysis of Hedda's conflicting personality traits, which she later described in detail in her book *Ibsen and the Actress*, has inspired many subsequent actresses to follow in her path. Interestingly, the majority of these belong to an English and American acting tradition in which the role of the actor is more important than that of the director. The list of English and American actresses who have offered a wide range of subtle and complex interpretations of Hedda's responses is impressive. It reads like a roll-call of those stars who helped to shape the acting styles of their generation in the theatres of London and New York:

Minnie Maddern Fiske at the Manhattan Theatre, New York, in 1903 and 1904; Mrs Patrick Campbell at the Court Theatre and then the Lyric Theatre, London, in 1907 and at the Everyman Theatre, London, in 1922; Eva Le Gallienne at the Civic Repertory Theatre, New York, in 1928, at the Broadhurst Theatre, New York, in 1934, and at the Cort Theatre, New York, in 1948; Jean Forbes-Robertson at the Criterion Theatre, London, in 1934 and 1936 and at the Arts Theatre, London, in 1951; Peggy Ashcroft at the Lyric Theatre, London, in 1954; Joan Greenwood at the New Arts Theatre and then St Martin's Theatre, London, in 1964; Maggie Smith at the Cambridge Theatre, London, in 1970; Claire Bloom at the Playhouse Theatre, New York, in 1971; Jill Bennett at the Royal Court Theatre, London, in 1972; Glenda Jackson at the Aldwych Theatre, London, in 1975; Janet Suzman at the Duke of York's Theatre, London, in 1977.

The intellectual and emotional preparation undertaken by all these actresses for the role of Hedda was as careful and detailed as that of Elizabeth Robins. Janet Suzman, for instance, has written a detailed account of how she prepared herself for her 1977 interpretation of

the role ('*Hedda Gabler*: the Play in Performance' in Errol
Durbach (ed.), *Ibsen and the Theatre*, pp. 88–92). She
looked carefully for all the clues to Hedda's behaviour
that Ibsen had littered throughout the text. She then
went on to build emotional scenarios for events that had
taken place before the action of the play, inventing, for
instance, a honeymoon itinerary. She then concentrated
on what she saw as the emotional core in Hedda's
character, namely her inability to live with compromise.
As a result of this, Hedda does and says things during
the play which have consequences that she cannot
foresee but which she is prepared to face. She takes
'terrific chances' but admits what she has done with
'disarming candour'. Her portrayal of Hedda's final
moments is based upon a clearly thought-through process
of understanding:

> Eilert's death, done with dignity, would have been a beacon
> to her. But he has only shown her how *not* to do it. Now
> she knows she has to take the whole burden on her own
> shoulders. They feel strangely less bowed as she does. A
> dread lightness comes upon her. Jokes come easily. (p.104)

Her interpretation is quite different from that of
Elizabeth Robins, but it is based upon the same process
of intuitive, intellectual and psychological analysis that
underpinned the work of the first great actress to take on
the challenge of presenting Hedda, in all her complexity,
to a theatre audience.

Radically different approaches to the play have
emerged in countries where directors rather than actors
dominate the theatre. In Russia, Sweden and Germany
leading directors at different points in the twentieth
century have presented their 'readings' of *Hedda Gabler*,
which have either been based on a deconstructive
interpretation of the play, or the wish to make an
aesthetic, philosophical or political comment on it. The
first example of this alternative approach may be found
in the 1906 production of the play by Meyerhold at
Vera Komisarjevskaya's Dramatic Theatre in St

Petersburg. Meyerhold's intention was to offer a deconstructive reading of the play, based on its inner symbolism. He stripped away all realistic detail. Using a narrow platform stage (as pioneered by the German director Georg Fuchs), Meyerhold showed a stage setting resonant with visual symbolism. The forestage was dominated by an armchair covered in white fur, which served as a throne for 'a cold, regal, autumnal Hedda'. The background showed a vista of blues and autumnal gold expressing the longings and inner mood of the central character. The acting was stylised. Often the actors used no moves or gestures, but instead spoke their lines straight out at the audience, relying on minimal changes of facial expression and eye movements to communicate subtexual meaning. This was an early example of pure director's theatre that fascinated some but antagonised others.*

Some sixty years later, another leading exponent of director's theatre, Ingmar Bergman, turned his attention to *Hedda Gabler* in his 1964 production of the play for Stockholm's Royal Dramatic Theatre. This was a production of much greater depth and significance than Meyerhold's early attempt at wrestling with the inner life of the play. Like Meyerhold, Bergman stripped the set of all unnecessary detail. He also, like Meyerhold, even dispensed with General Gabler's portrait. The muted maroon and black colours of the furniture and set reflected Hedda's dark state of mind. The set consisted of seven rehearsal screens covered in a dark maroon fabric. Another rehearsal screen divided the stage into two halves so that Hedda's private room could be shown stage right rather than upstage. This in turn permitted Gertrud Fridh, acting the role of Hedda, to respond silently (using gestures, facial expressions and moves) to what was said on stage. The set was airless and claustrophobic, and was reminiscent of the kind of setting

---

* For a detailed account of the production, see Edward Braun, *The Director and the Stage*, pp. 59–63. For an account of the response of contemporary critics, see Marker (1989), pp. 176–7.

one finds in Strindberg's late chamber plays. Bergman
seems to have viewed *Hedda Gabler* almost through the
eyes of Ibsen's arch rival, Strindberg. His reading of
*Hedda Gabler* transposed the play to the spiritual
landscape of Strindberg's *Ghost Sonata*. For him all the
characters were lost souls, imprisoned in an emotional
chamber of horrors. There was no trace of any positive
vision underpinning the work. Bergman showed us an
expressionist version of Hedda who had wandered into a
Strindbergian nightmare where tragedy has simply got
into the bloodstream. His Swedish actors conveyed this
vision with sculpted blocking patterns and a chiselled
intensity that was deeply impressive.

    When Bergman was invited by Sir Laurence Olivier to
revive his production in London in 1970 for the National
Theatre, he encountered some very real problems.
Bergman prefers to work with a trusted ensemble of
actors whom he knows well. In London, he was not
responsible for choosing his cast, and, in addition, he
found himself confronted by a group of actors who were
used to having a larger say in their approach to
character and interpretation than was the case in Sweden
and Germany. (In London in 1970, director's theatre was
a relatively new phenomenon.) Maggie Smith, for
instance, clearly insisted on establishing the emotional
motivation for her character's behaviour. This included,
in the opening scene, her miming Hedda succumbing to
an attack of morning sickness as she listened to Tesman
talking to his aunt in the next room. Bergman seems to
have found this action particularly grating. Maggie
Smith, however, as one of England's leading exponents
of high comedy acting, brought to her role an
unparalleled understanding of the comic texture of the
play and the dialogue. This is something Bergman had
largely sacrificed in Stockholm. London's critics preferred
her reading of the role to that of Bergman. Ronald
Bryden, for instance, wrote in the *Observer*:

    The maddening thing is that a naturalistic production would
    fit most of Maggie Smith's performance better. She is at her

best playing society's game: edging politeness with scornful artificiality, smiling with a sweetness which conceals daggers. Company brings a glittering, fragile glassiness to her manner. Every banal remark, every vulgar threat to her image of herself, sends a tiny shiver through her like a draft through a chandelier. At any moment you expect it to shatter. The threat of laceration, of splinters and blood, hangs in the air.

But when her poise does crack, there isn't the power behind it to evoke the beast whose real tragedy is simply that she comes of a larger, more predatory species than the silly herbivores around her; the force which can't be explained psychologically, but is simply, as Ibsen said, 'daemonic'. She conceals the deficiency with skill and speed. Plunging her fingers into Thea Elvsted's hair, darting for Eilert Loevborg's manuscript to thrust it into the stove, she achieves an electric, angular menace. But it's sleight of hand; hysteria, not self-declaration. Her Hedda remains Bergman's: a brilliant, pathetic case history. (5 July 1970)

Bergman did not enjoy his experience of working in London with English actors and has since worked exclusively with Swedish or German companies. His German version of *Hedda Gabler* for the Residenztheater, Munich, in 1979 went even further down the track of minimalist deconstruction. Stripped of all non-essential detail Bergman staged the work as a Strindbergian chamber play in one fluid act and without any intermission.*

Other German productions of *Hedda Gabler* during the 1970s tended to be postmodern commentaries on the play and its supposed values rather than sympathetic interpretations. In February 1977, Niels-Peter Rudolph presented a cabaret-style parody of the play at the Schiller Theatre in Berlin. The various characters in the piece wore ridiculous padded costumes and were all

* For a detailed account of the Stockholm and Munich productions, see Lise-Lone and Frederick J. Marker, *Ingmar Bergman. A Life in the Theater*, pp. 192–216.

mocked as grotesque stereotypes of bourgeois idiocy.
Peter Zadek's production of *Hedda Gabler* at Bochum in
the same month presented a more thoughtful critique of
the supposed bourgeois values underpinning the work. In
particular the setting, described as 'an orgy of velvet,
glass and marble', was conceived as a visual critique of
the high bourgeois social setting of the play (see Marker,
1989, pp. 193–5). By the end of the twentieth century,
the German theatre appeared to have come no closer to
an understanding of the subtlety and complexity of
Ibsen's play than at the end of the previous century. In
particular, what appears to have eluded German
directors and actors is any real understanding of the
comic undertow running through the whole play.

By comparison with heavy-handed teutonic parodies, a
somewhat more entertaining pastiche of *Hedda Gabler* was
put together by Charles Marowitz in his *Hedda Collage* of
1978 (published in 1982). This contrasted scenes from
the play with largely Freudian fantasy sequences (for
instance Hedda astride a giant phallic pistol that had
descended from the flies) and other erotic scenes in
which Loevborg is sucked off in Mademoiselle Danielle's
brothel, first by a half-naked prostitute and then briefly
by Hedda. Marowitz's aim was to show Hedda as an
emotional cripple because of her Electra complex.
Another entertaining experiment was tried in 1984 by
the American Ibsen Theatre who presented a production
of the play in drag with Charles Ludlam in the title role.
Obviously, *Hedda Gabler* as theatrical text has provoked
and stimulated practitioners into a wide range of fantasy-
based explorations.

Arguably, the one genuinely successful version of *Hedda
Gabler* based on the vision of an outstanding director
rather than the intuitive insight of actors, is the
production of the play directed in Stockholm by Ingmar
Bergman. Even in this case, however, one is left with the
uneasy feeling that Bergman has used all the magic
alchemy of his artistry to impose upon Ibsen's play an
essentially alien, Strindbergian reading of the text. Ibsen

did not share Strindberg's bleak view of the world and
he did not write plays to show characters clawing each
other pointlessly in an emotional torture chamber from
which there was no escape. (Ironically, Strindberg himself
violently disliked *Hedda Gabler*, because he was convinced
that he was the model for Eilert Loevborg.)

For directors and actors, as for readers, the challenge
posed by Ibsen in the theatre is to respond to the hidden
poetry between the lines of the theatre text. The
challenge is not met by resorting to cheap parody, or
grotesque burlesque, nor by imposing a subjective vision
onto the hidden poetic subtext that forcibly transposes it
into an alien landscape of the director's choice. The
challenge is instead to find creative ways of breathing
three-dimensional life into Ibsen's theatre poetry so that
audiences and actors can take delight in together sharing
its subtleties and complexities. Since the 1890s, some of
the leading actresses of the English and American stage
have responded to this challenge by offering their
audiences a series of magnificent interpretations of
Hedda's role. By comparison, the response of directors to
this challenge has been generally less impressive. Perhaps
this suggests that *Hedda Gabler* is ultimately a play for
actresses and actors rather than directors.

# Further Reading

## Collected editions of Ibsen's plays

*Samlede verker, hundreårsutgave*, 22 vols, edited by Halvdan Koht, Francis Bull and Didrik Arup Seip [with Ibsen's preliminary notes] (Oslo: Glydendal, 1928–58)

*The Oxford Ibsen*, 8 vols, edited by James McFarlane [with Ibsen's preliminary notes] (London: Oxford University Press, 1960–77)

*Ibsen Plays: 1–6*, translated and introduced by Michael Meyer (London: Methuen, 1980–7). Vol 1: *Ghosts, The Wild Duck, The Master Builder*; vol. 2: *A Doll's House, Enemy of the People, Hedda Gabler*; vol. 3: *Rosmersholm, The Lady from the Sea, Little Eyolf*; vol. 4: *The Pillars of Society, John Gabriel Borkman, When We Dead Awaken*; vol. 5: *Brand, Emperor and Galilean*; vol. 6: *Peer Gynt, The Pretenders*

## Studies of *Hedda Gabler* in English and Norwegian

Høst, Else, *Hedda Gabler. En monografi* [with an English summary] (Oslo: Aschehong, 1958)

Lyons, Charles R., *Hedda Gabler: Gender, Role and World* (Boston, Mass.: Twayne, 1991)

## Biographical studies of Ibsen

Beyer, Edvard, *Ibsen. The Man and his Work* (London: Souvenir Press, 1978)

Bryan, George B., *An Ibsen Companion: A Dictionary-guide to the Life, Works, and Critical Reception of Henrik Ibsen* (Westport, Conn. & London: Greenwood Press, 1984)

Gosse, Edmund, *Ibsen* (London: Hodder & Stoughton, 1907)

Ibsen, Bergliot, *The Three Ibsens* (London: Hutchinson, 1951)

Koht, Halvdan, *The Life of Ibsen*, 2 vols (London: Allen & Unwin, 1931)

Meyer, Michael, *Henrik Ibsen*, 3 vols (London: Hart-Davis, 1967–71)

Meyer, Michael, *Ibsen: A Biography* (Harmondsworth: Penguin, 1974)

## Critical approaches to Ibsen

*Late nineteenth-century criticism*

*William Archer on Ibsen. The Major Essays, 1889–1919*, edited by Thomas Postlewait (Westport, Conn., London: Greenwood, 1984)

Brandes, Georg, *Henrik Ibsen. A Critical Study* [1899] (New York: Benjamin Blom, 1964)

Egan, Michael (ed.), *Ibsen: The Critical Heritage* (London: Routlege & Kegan Paul, 1972)

Shaw, George Bernard, *The Quintessence of Ibsenism* (London: Walter Scott, 1891)

*Twentieth-century criticism*

Bradbrook, Muriel, *Ibsen the Norwegian: A Revaluation* (London: Chatto and Windus, 1966)

Chamberlain, J., *Ibsen, the Open Vision* (London: Athlone Press, 1982)

Fjelde, Rolf (ed.), *Ibsen. A Collection of Critical Essays* (Englewood Cliffs, NJ: Prentice-Hall, 1965)

Haakonsen, Daniel (ed.), *Contemporary Approaches to Ibsen*, vols 1–4 (Oslo: Oslo University Press, 1966–79)

Holtan, Orley, *Mythic Patterns in Ibsen's Last Plays* (Minneapolis: University of Minnesota Press, 1970)

Hurt, James, *Catiline's Dream: An Essay on Ibsen's Plays* (Urbana: University of Illinois Press, 1972)

Lyons, Charles R., *Henrik Ibsen. The Divided Consciousness* (Carbondale: Southern Illinois University Press, 1972)

McFarlane, James, *Ibsen and the Temper of Norwegian*

*Literature* (London: Oxford University Press, 1960)

McFarlane, James, *Henrik Ibsen: A Critical Anthology* (Harmondsworth: Penguin, 1970)

McFarlane, James, *The Cambridge Companion to Ibsen* (Cambridge: Cambridge University Press, 1994)

Northam, John, *Ibsen's Dramatic Method: A Study of the Prose Dramas* (Oslo: Oslo University Press, 1971)

Northam, John, *Ibsen. A Critical Study* (Cambridge: Cambridge University Press, 1973)

Tennant, P. F. D., *Ibsen's Dramatic Technique* (Cambridge: Bowes & Bowes, 1948)

Thomas, David, *Henrik Ibsen* (London: Macmillan, 1983)

Weigand, H. J., *The Modern Ibsen* (London: Dent, 1925)

Williams, Raymond, *Drama from Ibsen to Eliot* (Harmondsworth: Peregrine Books, 1952)

## Ibsen and the theatre

Braun, Edward, *The Director and the Stage* (London: Methuen, 1982)

Durbach, E. (ed.), *Ibsen and the Theatre* (London: Macmillan, 1980)

Marker, Frederick and Lise-Lone, *Ibsen's Lively Art. A Performance Study of the Major Plays* (Cambridge: Cambridge University Press, 1989)

Marker, Frederick and Lise-Lone, *Ingmar Bergman. A Life in the Theater* (Cambridge: Cambridge University Press, 1992)

Marker, Frederick and Lise-Lone, *The Scandinavian Theatre: A Short History* (Oxford: Basil Blackwell, 1975)

Robins, Elizabeth, *Ibsen and the Actress* (London: L. & V. Woolfe, 1928)

# Hedda Gabler

*translated by Michael Meyer*

This translation of *Hedda Gabler* was first performed on 9 November 1960 at the 4th Street Theatre, New York, in a production by David Ross with Anne Meacham as Hedda. The first London performance was on 29 June 1970 at the Cambridge Theatre, under the auspices of the National Theatre. The cast was:

| | |
|---|---|
| **George Tesman**, *research graduate in cultural history* | Jeremy Brett |
| **Hedda Tesman**, *his wife* | Maggie Smith |
| **Miss Juliana Tesman**, *his aunt* | Jeanne Watts |
| **Mrs Elvsted** | Sheila Reid |
| **Judge Brack** | John Moffat |
| **Eilert Loevborg** | Robert Stephens |
| **Bertha**, *a maid* | Julia McCarthy |

*Directed by* Ingmar Bergman

The action takes place in **Tesman**'s villa in the fashionable quarter of town.

# Act One

*A large drawing-room, handsomely and tastefully furnished; decorated
in dark colours. In the rear wall is a broad open doorway, with
curtains drawn back to either side. It leads to a smaller room,
decorated in the same style as the drawing-room. In the right-hand
wall of the drawing-room a folding door leads out to the hall. The
opposite wall, on the left, contains french windows, also with curtains
drawn back on either side. Through the glass we can see part of a
veranda, and trees in autumn colours. Downstage stands an oval table,
covered by a cloth and surrounded by chairs. Downstage right, against
the wall, is a broad stove tiled with dark porcelain; in front of it
stand a high-backed armchair, a cushioned footrest and two footstools.
Upstage right, in an alcove, is a corner sofa, with a small, round
table. Downstage left, a little away from the wall, is another sofa.
Upstage of the french windows, a piano. On either side of the open
doorway in the rear wall stand what-nots holding ornaments of terra-
cotta and majolica. Against the rear wall of the smaller room can be
seen a sofa, a table and a couple of chairs. Above this sofa hangs the
portrait of a handsome old man in general's uniform. Above the table
a lamp hangs from the ceiling, with a shade of opalescent, milky
glass. All round the drawing-room bunches of flowers stand in vases
and glasses. More bunches lie on the tables. The floors of both rooms
are covered with thick carpets. Morning light. The sun shines in
through the french windows.*

**Miss Juliana Tesman**, *wearing a hat and carrying a parasol,
enters from the hall, followed by* **Bertha**, *who is carrying a bunch
of flowers wrapped in paper.* **Miss Tesman** *is about sixty-five, of
pleasant and kindly appearance. She is neatly but simply dressed in
grey outdoor clothes.* **Bertha**, *the maid, is rather simple and rustic-
looking. She is getting on in years.*

**Miss Tesman** (*stops just inside the door, listens, and says in a
hushed voice*)  Well, fancy that! They're not up yet!

**Bertha** (*also in hushed tones*)  What did I tell you, miss? The
boat didn't get in till midnight. And when they did turn up
– Jesus, miss, you should have seen all the things madam

made me unpack before she'd go to bed!

**Miss Tesman**   Ah, well. Let them have a good lie in. But let's have some nice fresh air waiting for them when they do come down. (*Goes to the french windows and throws them wide open.*)

**Bertha** (*bewildered at the table, the bunch of flowers in her hand*)   I'm blessed if there's a square inch left to put anything. I'll have to let it lie here, miss. (*Puts it on the piano.*)

**Miss Tesman**   Well, Bertha dear, so now you have a new mistress. Heaven knows it nearly broke my heart to have to part with you.

**Bertha** (*snivels*)   What about me, Miss Juju? How do you suppose I felt? After all the happy years I've spent with you and Miss Rena?

**Miss Tesman**   We must accept it bravely, Bertha. It was the only way. George needs you to take care of him. He could never manage without you. You've looked after him ever since he was a tiny boy.

**Bertha**   Oh, but, Miss Juju, I can't help thinking about Miss Rena, lying there all helpless, poor dear. And that new girl! She'll never learn the proper way to handle an invalid.

**Miss Tesman**   Oh, I'll manage to train her. I'll do most of the work myself, you know. You needn't worry about my poor sister, Bertha dear.

**Bertha**   But, Miss Juju, there's another thing. I'm frightened madam may not find me suitable.

**Miss Tesman**   Oh, nonsense, Bertha. There may be one or two little things to begin with –

**Bertha**   She's a real lady. Wants everything just so.

**Miss Tesman**   But of course she does! General Gabler's daughter! Think of what she was accustomed to when the general was alive. You remember how we used to see her

out riding with her father? In that long black skirt? With
the feather in her hat?

**Bertha**   Oh, yes, miss. As if I could forget! But, Lord! I
never dreamed I'd live to see a match between her and
Master Georgie.

**Miss Tesman**   Neither did I. By the way, Bertha, from
now on you must stop calling him Master Georgie. You
must say Dr Tesman.

**Bertha**   Yes, madam said something about that too. Last
night – the moment they'd set foot inside the door. Is it
true, then, miss?

**Miss Tesman**   Indeed it is. Just fancy, Bertha, some
foreigners have made him a doctor. It happened while they
were away. I had no idea till he told me when they got off
the boat.

**Bertha**   Well, I suppose there's no limit to what he won't
become. He's that clever. I never thought he'd go in for
hospital work, though.

**Miss Tesman**   No, he's not that kind of doctor. (*Nods
impressively.*) In any case, you may soon have to address him
by an even grander title.

**Bertha**   You don't say! What might that be, miss?

**Miss Tesman** (*smiles*)   Ah! If you only knew! (*Moved.*)
Dear God, if only poor Joachim could rise out of his grave
and see what his little son has grown into! (*Looks round.*) But,
Bertha, why have you done this? Taken the chintz covers
off all the furniture!

*bright colour cotton*

**Bertha**   Madam said I was to. Can't stand chintz covers
on chairs, she said.

**Miss Tesman**   But surely they're not going to use this
room as a parlour?

**Bertha**   So I gathered, miss. From what madam said. He
didn't say anything. The Doctor.

**George Tesman** *comes into the rear room from the right, humming, with an open, empty travelling-bag in his hand. He is about thirty-three, of medium height and youthful appearance, rather plump, with an open, round, contented face, and fair hair and beard. He wears spectacles, and is dressed in comfortable indoor clothes.*

**Miss Tesman**   Good morning! Good morning, George!

**Tesman** (*in open doorway*)   Auntie Juju! Dear Auntie Juju! (*Comes forward and shakes her hand.*) You've come all the way out here! And so early! What?

**Miss Tesman**   Well, I had to make sure you'd settled in comfortably.

**Tesman**   But you can't have had a proper night's sleep.

**Miss Tesman**   Oh, never mind that.

**Tesman**   But you got home safely?

**Miss Tesman**   Oh, yes. Judge Brack kindly saw me home.

**Tesman**   We were so sorry we couldn't give you a lift. But you saw how it was – Hedda had so much luggage – and she insisted on having it all with her.

**Miss Tesman**   Yes, I've never seen so much luggage.

**Bertha** (*to* **Tesman**)   Shall I go and ask madam if there's anything I can lend her a hand with?

**Tesman**   Er – thank you, Bertha, no, you needn't bother. She says if she wants you for anything she'll ring.

**Bertha** (*over to right*)   Oh. Very good.

**Tesman**   Oh, Bertha – take this bag, will you?

**Bertha** (*takes it*)   I'll put it in the attic. (*Goes.*)

**Tesman**   Just fancy, Auntie Juju, I filled that whole bag with notes for my book. You know, it's really incredible what I've managed to find rooting through those archives. By Jove! Wonderful old things no one even knew existed –

**Miss Tesman**   I'm sure you didn't waste a single moment of your honeymoon, George dear.

**Tesman**   No, I think I can truthfully claim that. But, Auntie Juju, do take your hat off. Here. Let me untie it for you. What?

**Miss Tesman** (*as he does so*)   Oh dear, oh dear! It's just as if you were still living at home with us.

**Tesman** (*turns the hat in his hand and looks at it*)   I say! What a splendid new hat!

**Miss Tesman**   I bought it for Hedda's sake.

**Tesman**   For Hedda's sake? What?

**Miss Tesman**   So that Hedda needn't be ashamed of me, in case we ever go for a walk together.

**Tesman** (*pats her cheek*)   You still think of everything, don't you, Auntie Juju? (*Puts the hat down on a chair by the table.*) Come on, let's sit down here on the sofa. And have a little chat while we wait for Hedda.

*They sit. She puts her parasol in the corner of the sofa.*

**Miss Tesman** (*clasps both his hands and looks at him*)   Oh, George, it's so wonderful to have you back, and to be able to see you with my own eyes again! Poor dear Joachim's own son!

**Tesman**   What about me? It's wonderful for me to see you again, Auntie Juju. You've been a mother to me. And a father, too.

**Miss Tesman**   You'll always keep a soft spot in your heart for your old aunties, won't you, George dear?

**Tesman**   I suppose Auntie Rena's no better? What?

**Miss Tesman**   Alas, no. I'm afraid she'll never get better, poor dear. She's lying there just as she has for all these years. Please God I may be allowed to keep her for a little longer. If I lost her I don't know what I'd do. Especially now I haven't you to look after.

**Tesman** (*pats her on the back*)   There, there, there!

**Miss Tesman** (*with a sudden change of mood*)   Oh, but, George, fancy you being a married man! And to think it's you who've won Hedda Gabler! The beautiful Hedda Gabler! Fancy! She was always so surrounded by admirers.

**Tesman** (*hums a little and smiles contentedly*)   Yes, I suppose there are quite a few people in this town who wouldn't mind being in my shoes. What?

**Miss Tesman**   And what a honeymoon! Five months! Nearly six.

**Tesman**   Well, I've done a lot of work, you know. All those archives to go through. And I've had to read lots of books.

**Miss Tesman**   Yes, dear, of course. (*Lowers her voice confidentially.*) But tell me, George – haven't you any – any extra little piece of news to give me?

**Tesman**   You mean, arising out of the honeymoon?

**Miss Tesman**   Yes.

**Tesman**   No, I don't think there's anything I didn't tell you in my letters. My doctorate, of course – but I told you about that last night, didn't I?

**Miss Tesman**   Yes, yes, I didn't mean that kind of thing. I was just wondering – are you – are you expecting – ?

**Tesman**   Expecting what?

**Miss Tesman**   Oh, come on, George, I'm your old aunt!

**Tesman**   Well, actually – yes, I am expecting something.

**Miss Tesman**   I knew it!

**Tesman**   You'll be happy to learn that before very long I expect to become a – professor.

**Miss Tesman**   Professor?

**Tesman**   I think I may say that the matter has been

decided. But, Auntie Juju, you know about this.

**Miss Tesman** (*gives a little laugh*)  Yes, of course. I'd forgotten. (*Changes her tone.*) But we were talking about your honeymoon. It must have cost a dreadful amount of money, George?

**Tesman**  Oh well, you know, that big research grant I got helped a good deal.

**Miss Tesman**  But how on earth did you manage to make it do for two?

**Tesman**  Well, to tell the truth it was a bit tricky. What?

**Miss Tesman**  Especially when one's travelling with a lady. A little bird tells me that makes things very much more expensive.

**Tesman**  Well, yes, of course it does make things a little more expensive. But Hedda has to do things in style, Auntie Juju. I mean, she has to. Anything less grand wouldn't have suited her.

**Miss Tesman**  No, no, I suppose not. A honeymoon abroad seems to be the vogue nowadays. But tell me, have you had time to look round the house?

**Tesman**  You bet. I've been up since the crack of dawn.

**Miss Tesman**  Well, what do you think of it?

**Tesman**  Splendid. Absolutely splendid. I'm only wondering what we're going to do with those two empty rooms between that little one and Hedda's bedroom.

**Miss Tesman** (*laughs slyly*)  Ah, George, dear, I'm sure you'll manage to find some use for them – in time.

**Tesman**  Yes, of course, Auntie Juju, how stupid of me. You're thinking of my books? What?

**Miss Tesman**  Yes, yes, dear boy. I was thinking of your books.

**Tesman**  You know, I'm so happy for Hedda's sake that

we've managed to get this house. Before we became engaged she often used to say this was the only house in town she felt she could really bear to live in. It used to belong to Mrs Falk – you know, the Prime Minister's widow.

**Miss Tesman**   Fancy that! And what a stroke of luck it happened to come into the market. Just as you'd left on your honeymoon.

**Tesman**   Yes, Auntie Juju, we've certainly had all the luck with us. What?

**Miss Tesman**   But, George dear, the expense! It's going to make a dreadful hole in your pocket, all this.

**Tesman** (*a little downcast*)   Yes, I – I suppose it will, won't it?

**Miss Tesman**   Oh, George, really!

**Tesman**   How much do you think it'll cost? Roughly, I mean? What?

**Miss Tesman**   I can't possibly say till I see the bills.

**Tesman**   Well, luckily Judge Brack's managed to get it on very favourable terms. He wrote and told Hedda so.

**Miss Tesman**   Don't you worry, George dear. Anyway, I've stood security for all the furniture and carpets.

**Tesman**   Security? But dear, sweet Auntie Juju, how could you possibly stand security?

**Miss Tesman**   I've arranged a mortgage on our annuity.

**Tesman** (*jumps up*)   What? On your annuity? And – Auntie Rena's?

**Miss Tesman**   Yes. Well, I couldn't think of any other way.

**Tesman** (*stands in front of her*)   Auntie Juju, have you gone completely out of your mind? That annuity's all you and Auntie Rena have.

**Miss Tesman**  All right, there's no need to get so excited about it. It's a pure formality, you know. Judge Brack told me so. He was so kind as to arrange it all for me. A pure formality; those were his very words.

**Tesman**  I dare say. All the same –

**Miss Tesman**  Anyway, you'll have a salary of your own now. And, good heavens, even if we did have to fork out a little – tighten our belts for a week or two – why, we'd be happy to do so for your sake.

**Tesman**  Oh, Auntie Juju! Will you never stop sacrificing yourself for me?

**Miss Tesman**  (*gets up and puts her hands on his shoulders*) What else have I to live for but to smooth your road a little, my dear boy? You've never had any mother or father to turn to. And now at last we've achieved our goal. I won't deny we've had our little difficulties now and then. But now, thank the good Lord, George dear, all your worries are past.

**Tesman**  Yes, it's wonderful really how everything's gone just right for me.

**Miss Tesman**  Yes! And the enemies who tried to bar your way have been struck down. They have been made to bite the dust. The man who was your most dangerous rival has had the mightiest fall. And now he's lying there in the pit he dug for himself, poor misguided creature.

**Tesman**  Have you heard any news of Eilert? Since I went away?

**Miss Tesman**  Only that he's said to have published a new book.

**Tesman**  What! Eilert Loevborg? You mean – just recently? What?

**Miss Tesman**  So they say. I don't imagine it can be of any value, do you? When your new book comes out, that'll be another story. What's it going to be about?

**Tesman**   The domestic industries of Brabant in the Middle Ages.

**Miss Tesman**   Oh, George! The things you know about!

**Tesman**   Mind you, it may be some time before I actually get down to writing it. I've made these very extensive notes, and I've got to file and index them first.

**Miss Tesman**   Ah, yes! Making notes; filing and indexing; you've always been wonderful at that. Poor dear Joachim was just the same.

**Tesman**   I'm looking forward so much to getting down to that. Especially now I've a home of my own to work in.

**Miss Tesman**   And above all, now that you have the girl you set your heart on, George dear.

**Tesman** (*embraces her*)   Oh, yes, Auntie Juju, yes! Hedda's the loveliest thing of all! (*Looks towards the doorway.*) I think I hear her coming. What?

**Hedda** *enters the rear room from the left, and comes into the drawing-room. She is a woman of* twenty-nine. *Distinguished, aristocratic face and figure. Her complexion is pale and opalescent. Her eyes are steel-grey, with an expression of cold, calm serenity. Her hair is of a handsome auburn colour, but is not especially abundant. She is dressed in an elegant, somewhat loose-fitting morning gown.*

**Miss Tesman** (*goes to greet her*)   Good morning, Hedda dear! Good morning!

**Hedda** (*holds out her hand*)   Good morning, dear Miss Tesman. What an early hour to call. So kind of you.

**Miss Tesman** (*seems somewhat embarrassed*)   And has the young bride slept well in her new home?

**Hedda**   Oh – thank you, yes. Passably well.

**Tesman** (*laughs*)   Passably? I say. Hedda, that's good! When I jumped out of bed, you were sleeping like a top.

**Hedda**   Yes. Fortunately. One has to accustom oneself to anything new, Miss Tesman. It takes time. (*Looks left.*) Oh,

that maid's left the french windows open. This room's flooded with sun.

**Miss Tesman** (*goes towards the windows*)  Oh – let me close them.

**Hedda**  No, no, don't do that. Tesman dear, draw the curtains. This light's blinding me.

**Tesman** (*at the windows*)  Yes, yes, dear. There, Hedda, now you've got shade and fresh air.

**Hedda**  This room needs fresh air. All these flowers – ! But my dear Miss Tesman, won't you take a seat?

**Miss Tesman**  No, really not, thank you. I just wanted to make sure you have everything you need. I must see about getting back home. My poor dear sister will be waiting for me.

**Tesman**  Be sure to give her my love, won't you? Tell her I'll run over and see her later today.

**Miss Tesman**  Oh yes, I'll tell her that. Oh, George – (*Fumbles in the pocket of her skirt.*) I almost forgot. I've brought something for you.

**Tesman**  What's that, Auntie Juju? What?

**Miss Tesman** (*pulls out a flat package wrapped in newspaper and gives it to him*)  Open and see, dear boy.

**Tesman** (*opens the package*)  Good heavens! Auntie Juju, you've kept them! Hedda, this is really very touching. What?

**Hedda** (*by the what-nots, on the right*)  What is it, Tesman?

**Tesman**  My old shoes! My slippers, Hedda!

**Hedda**  Oh, them. I remember you kept talking about them on our honeymoon.

**Tesman**  Yes, I missed them dreadfully. (*Goes over to her.*) Here, Hedda, take a look.

**Hedda** (*goes away towards the stove*)  Thanks, I won't bother.

**Tesman** (*follows her*) Fancy, Hedda, Auntie Rena's embroidered them for me. Despite her being so ill. Oh, you can't imagine what memories they have for me.

**Hedda** (*by the table*) Not for me.

**Miss Tesman** No, Hedda's right there, George.

**Tesman** Yes, but I thought since she's one of the family now –

**Hedda** (*interrupts*) Tesman, we really can't go on keeping this maid.

**Miss Tesman** Not keep Bertha?

**Tesman** What makes you say that, dear? What?

**Hedda** (*points*) Look at that! She's left her old hat lying on the chair.

**Tesman** (*appalled, drops his slippers on the floor*) But, Hedda –!

**Hedda** Suppose someone came in and saw it?

**Tesman** But, Hedda – that's Auntie Juju's hat.

**Hedda** Oh?

**Miss Tesman** (*picks up the hat*) Indeed it's mine. And it doesn't happen to be old, Hedda dear.

**Hedda** I didn't look at it very closely, Miss Tesman.

**Miss Tesman** (*trying on the hat*) As a matter of fact, it's the first time I've worn it. As the good Lord is my witness.

**Tesman** It's very pretty, too. Really smart.

**Miss Tesman** Oh, I'm afraid it's nothing much really. (*Looks round.*) My parasol. Ah, there it is. (*Takes it.*) This is mine, too. (*Murmurs.*) Not Bertha's.

**Tesman** A new hat and a new parasol! I say, Hedda, fancy that!

**Hedda** Very pretty and charming.

**Tesman**    Yes, isn't it? What? But, Auntie Juju, take a good look at Hedda before you go. Isn't she pretty and charming?

**Miss Tesman**    Dear boy, there's nothing new in that. Hedda's been a beauty ever since the day she was born. (*Nods and goes right.*)

**Tesman** (*follows her*)    Yes, but have you noticed how strong and healthy she's looking? And how she's filled out since we went away?

**Miss Tesman** (*stops and turns*)    Filled out?

**Hedda** (*walks across the room*)    Oh, can't we forget it?

**Tesman**    Yes, Auntie Juju – you can't see it so clearly with that dress on. But I've good reason to know –

**Hedda** (*by the french windows, impatiently*)    You haven't good reason to know anything.

**Tesman**    It must have been the mountain air up there in the Tyrol –

**Hedda** (*curtly, interrupts him*)    I'm exactly the same as when I went away.

**Tesman**    You keep on saying so. But you're not. I'm right, aren't I, Auntie Juju?

**Miss Tesman** (*has folded her hands and is gazing at her*) She's beautiful – beautiful. Hedda is beautiful. (*Goes over to* **Hedda**, *takes her head between her hands, draws it down and kisses her hair.*) God bless and keep you, Hedda Tesman. For George's sake.

**Hedda** (*frees herself politely*)    Oh – let me go, please.

**Miss Tesman** (*quietly, emotionally*)    I shall come and see you both every day.

**Tesman**    Yes, Auntie Juju, please do. What?

**Miss Tesman**    Goodbye! Goodbye!

*She goes out into the hall.* **Tesman** *follows her. The door remains*

*open.* **Tesman** *is heard sending his love to* **Aunt Rena** *and thanking* **Miss Tesman** *for his slippers. Meanwhile* **Hedda** *walks up and down the room, raising her arms and clenching her fists as though in desperation. Then she throws aside the curtains from the french windows and stands there, looking out. A few moments later* **Tesman** *returns and closes the door behind him.*

**Tesman** (*picks up his slippers from the floor*)  What are you looking at, Hedda?

**Hedda** (*calm and controlled again*)  Only the leaves. They're so golden and withered.

**Tesman** (*wraps up the slippers and lays them on the table*) Well, we're in September now.

**Hedda** (*restless again*)  Yes. We're already into September.

**Tesman**  Auntie Juju was behaving rather oddly, I thought, didn't you? Almost as though she was in church or something. I wonder what came over her. Any idea?

**Hedda**  I hardly know her. Does she often act like that?

**Tesman**  Not to the extent she did today.

**Hedda** (*goes away from the french windows*)  Do you think she was hurt by what I said about the hat?

**Tesman**  Oh, I don't think so. A little at first, perhaps –

**Hedda**  But what a thing to do, throw her hat down in someone's drawing-room. People don't do such things.

**Tesman**  I'm sure Auntie Juju doesn't do it very often.

**Hedda**  Oh well, I'll make it up with her.

**Tesman**  Oh Hedda, would you?

**Hedda**  When you see them this afternoon invite her to come out here this evening.

**Tesman**  You bet I will! I say, there's another thing which would please her enormously.

**Hedda**  Oh?

**Tesman**   If you could bring yourself to call her Auntie Juju. For my sake, Hedda? What?

**Hedda**   Oh no, really, Tesman, you mustn't ask me to do that. I've told you so once before. I'll try to call her Aunt Juliana. That's as far as I'll go.

**Tesman** (*after a moment*)   I say, Hedda, is anything wrong? What?

**Hedda**   I'm just looking at my old piano. It doesn't really go with all this.

**Tesman**   As soon as I start getting my salary we'll see about changing it.

**Hedda**   No, no, don't let's change it. I don't want to part with it. We can move it into that little room and get another one to put in here.

**Tesman** (*a little downcast*)   Yes, we – might do that.

**Hedda** (*picks up the bunch of flowers from the piano*)   These flowers weren't here when we arrived last night.

**Tesman**   I expect Auntie Juju brought them.

**Hedda**   Here's a card. (*Takes it out and reads.*) 'Will come back later today.' Guess who it's from?

**Tesman**   No idea. Who? What?

**Hedda**   It says: 'Mrs Elvsted.'

**Tesman**   No, really? Mrs Elvsted! She used to be Miss Rysing, didn't she?

**Hedda**   Yes. She was the one with that irritating hair she was always showing off. I hear she used to be an old flame of yours.

**Tesman** (*laughs*)   That didn't last long. Anyway, that was before I got to know you, Hedda. By Jove, fancy her being in town!

**Hedda**   Strange she should call. I only knew her at school.

**Tesman**   Yes, I haven't seen her for – oh, heaven knows how long. I don't know how she manages to stick it out up there in the north. What?

**Hedda** (*thinks for a moment, then says suddenly*)   Tell me, Tesman, doesn't he live somewhere up in those parts? You know – Eilert Loevborg?

**Tesman**   Yes, that's right. So he does.

**Bertha** *enters from the hall.*

**Bertha**   She's here again, madam. The lady who came and left the flowers. (*Points.*) The ones you're holding.

**Hedda**   Oh, is she? Well, show her in.

**Bertha** *opens the door for* **Mrs Elvsted** *and goes out.* **Mrs Elvsted** *is a delicately built woman with gentle, attractive features. Her eyes are light blue, large, and somewhat prominent, with a frightened, questioning expression. Her hair is extremely fair, almost flaxen, and is exceptionally wavy and abundant. She is two or three years younger than* **Hedda**. *She is wearing a dark visiting dress, in good taste but not quite in the latest fashion.*

**Hedda** (*goes cordially to greet her*)   Dear Mrs Elvsted, good morning! How delightful to see you again after all this time!

**Mrs Elvsted** (*nervously, trying to control herself*)   Yes, it's many years since we met.

**Tesman**   And since *we* met. What?

**Hedda**   Thank you for your lovely flowers.

**Mrs Elvsted**   I wanted to come yesterday afternoon. But they told me you were away –

**Tesman**   You've only just arrived in town, then? What?

**Mrs Elvsted**   I got here yesterday, around midday. Oh, I became almost desperate when I heard you weren't here.

**Hedda**   Desperate? Why?

**Tesman**   My dear Mrs Rysing – Elvsted –

**Hedda**   There's nothing wrong, I hope?

**Mrs Elvsted**   Yes, there is. And I don't know anyone else here whom I can turn to.

**Hedda** (*puts the flowers down on the table*)   Come and sit with me on the sofa –

**Mrs Elvsted**   Oh, I feel too restless to sit down.

**Hedda**   You must. Come along, now.

*She pulls* **Mrs Elvsted** *down on to the sofa and sits beside her.*

**Tesman**   Well? Tell us, Mrs – er –

**Hedda**   Has something happened at home?

**Mrs Elvsted**   Yes – that is, yes and no. Oh, I do hope you won't misunderstand me –

**Hedda**   Then you'd better tell us the whole story, Mrs Elvsted.

**Tesman**   That's why you've come. What?

**Mrs Elvsted**   Yes – yes, it is. Well, then – in case you don't already know – Eilert Loevborg is in town.

**Hedda**   Loevborg here?

**Tesman**   Eilert back in town? Fancy, Hedda, did you hear that?

**Hedda**   Yes, of course I heard.

**Mrs Elvsted**   He's been here a week. A whole week! In this city. Alone. With all those dreadful people –

**Hedda**   But, my dear Mrs Elvsted, what concern is he of yours?

**Mrs Elvsted** (*gives her a frightened look and says quickly*)   He's been tutoring the children.

**Hedda**   Your children?

**Mrs Elvsted**   My husband's. I have none.

**Hedda**   Oh, you mean your stepchildren.

**Mrs Elvsted**   Yes.

**Tesman** (*gropingly*)   But was he sufficiently – I don't know how to put it – sufficiently regular in his habits to be suited to such a post? What?

**Mrs Elvsted**   For the past two to three years he has been living irreproachably.

**Tesman**   You don't say! Hedda, do you hear that?

**Hedda**   I hear.

**Mrs Elvsted**   Quite irreproachably, I assure you. In every respect. All the same – in this big city – with money in his pockets – I'm so dreadfully frightened something may happen to him.

**Tesman**   But why didn't he stay up there with you and your husband?

**Mrs Elvsted**   Once his book had come out, he became restless.

**Tesman**   Oh, yes – Auntie Juju said he's brought out a new book.

**Mrs Elvsted**   Yes, a big new book about the history of civilization. A kind of general survey. It came out a fortnight ago. Everyone's been buying it and reading it – it's created a tremendous stir –

**Tesman**   Has it really? It must be something he's dug up, then.

**Mrs Elvsted**   You mean from the old days?

**Tesman**   Yes.

**Mrs Elvsted**   No, he's written it all since he came to live with us.

**Tesman**   Well, that's splendid news, Hedda. Fancy that!

**Mrs Elvsted**   Oh, yes! If only he can go on like this!

**Hedda**  Have you met him since you came here?

**Mrs Elvsted**  No, not yet. I had such dreadful difficulty finding his address. But this morning I managed to track him down at last.

**Hedda** (*looks searchingly at her*)  I must say I find it a little strange that your husband – hm –

**Mrs Elvsted** (*starts nervously*)  My husband! What do you mean?

**Hedda**  That he should send you all the way here on an errand of this kind. I'm surprised he didn't come himself to keep an eye on his friend.

**Mrs Elvsted**  Oh, no, no – my husband hasn't the time. Besides, I – er – wanted to do some shopping here.

**Hedda** (*with a slight smile*)  Ah. Well, that's different.

**Mrs Elvsted** (*gets up quickly, restlessly*)  Please, Mr Tesman, I beg you – be kind to Eilert Loevborg if he comes here. I'm sure he will. I mean, you used to be such good friends in the old days. And you're both studying the same subject, as far as I can understand. You're in the same field, aren't you?

**Tesman**  Well, we used to be, anyway.

**Mrs Elvsted**  Yes – so I beg you earnestly, do please, please, keep an eye on him. Oh, Mr Tesman, do promise me you will.

**Tesman**  I shall be only too happy to do so, Mrs Rysing.

**Hedda**  Elvsted.

**Tesman**  I'll do everything for Eilert that lies in my power. You can rely on that.

**Mrs Elvsted**  Oh, how good and kind you are! (*Presses his hands.*) Thank you, thank you, thank you. (*Frightened.*) My husband's so fond of him, you see.

**Hedda** (*gets up*)  You'd better send him a note, Tesman.

He may not come to you of his own accord.

**Tesman**   Yes, that'd probably be the best plan, Hedda. What?

**Hedda**   The sooner the better. Why not do it now?

**Mrs Elvsted** (*pleadingly*)   Oh yes, if only you would.

**Tesman**   I'll do it this very moment. Do you have his address, Mrs – er – Elvsted?

**Mrs Elvsted**   Yes. (*Takes a small piece of paper from her pocket and gives it to him.*)

**Tesman**   Good, good. Right, well, I'll go inside and – (*Looks round.*) Where are my slippers? Oh yes, here. (*Picks up the package and is about to go.*)

**Hedda**   Try to sound friendly. Make it a nice long letter.

**Tesman**   Right, I will.

**Mrs Elvsted**   Please don't say anything about my having seen you.

**Tesman**   Good heavens, no, of course not. What?

*He goes out through the rear room to the right.*

**Hedda** (*goes over to* **Mrs Elvsted***, smiles, and says softly*) Well! Now we've killed two birds with one stone.

**Mrs Elvsted**   What do you mean?

**Hedda**   Didn't you realize I wanted to get him out of the room?

**Mrs Elvsted**   So that he could write the letter?

**Hedda**   And so that I could talk to you alone.

**Mrs Elvsted** (*confused*)   About this?

**Hedda**   Yes, about this.

**Mrs Elvsted** (*in alarm*)   But there's nothing more to tell, Mrs Tesman. Really there isn't.

**Hedda**    Oh, yes, there is. There's a lot more. I can see that. Come along, let's sit down and have a little chat.

*She pushes* **Mrs Elvsted** *down into the armchair by the stove and seats herself on one of the footstools.*

**Mrs Elvsted** (*looks anxiously at her watch*)    Really, Mrs Tesman, I think I ought to be going now.

**Hedda**    There's no hurry. Well? How are things at home?

**Mrs Elvsted**    I'd rather not speak about that.

**Hedda**    But, my dear, you can tell me. Good heavens, we were at school together.

**Mrs Elvsted**    Yes, but you were a year senior to me. Oh, I used to be terribly frightened of you in those days.

**Hedda**    Frightened of me?

**Mrs Elvsted**    Yes, terribly frightened. Whenever you met me on the staircase you used to pull my hair.

**Hedda**    No, did I?

**Mrs Elvsted**    Yes. And once you said you'd burn it all off.

**Hedda**    Oh, that was only in fun.

**Mrs Elvsted**    Yes, but I was so silly in those days. And then afterwards – I mean, we've drifted so far apart. Our backgrounds were so different.

**Hedda**    Well, now we must try to drift together again. Now listen. When we were at school we used to call each other by our Christian names –

**Mrs Elvsted**    No, I'm sure you're mistaken.

**Hedda**    I'm sure I'm not. I remember it quite clearly. Let's tell each other our secrets, as we used to in the old days. (*Moves closer on her footstool.*) There, now. (*Kisses her on the cheek.*) You must call me Hedda.

**Mrs Elvsted** (*squeezes her hands and pats them*)    Oh, you're

so kind. I'm not used to people being so nice to me.

**Hedda**   Now, now, now. And I shall call you Tora, the way I used to.

**Mrs Elvsted**   My name is Thea.

**Hedda**   Yes, of course. Of course. I meant Thea. (*Looks at her sympathetically.*) So you're not used to kindness, Thea? In your own home?

**Mrs Elvsted**   Oh, if only I had a home! But I haven't. I've never had one.

**Hedda** (*looks at her for a moment*)   I thought that was it.

**Mrs Elvsted** (*stares blankly and helplessly*)   Yes – yes – yes.

**Hedda**   I can't remember exactly, but didn't you first go to Mr Elvsted as a housekeeper?

**Mrs Elvsted**   Governess, actually. But his wife – at the time, I mean – she was an invalid, and had to spend most of her time in bed. So I had to look after the house, too.

**Hedda**   But in the end, you became mistress of the house.

**Mrs Elvsted** (*sadly*)   Yes, I did.

**Hedda**   Let me see. Roughly how long ago was that?

**Mrs Elvsted**   When I got married, you mean?

**Hedda**   Yes.

**Mrs Elvsted**   About five years.

**Hedda**   Yes; it must be about that.

**Mrs Elvsted**   Oh, those fives years! Especially the last two or three. Oh, Mrs Tesman, if you only knew – !

**Hedda** (*slaps her hand gently*)   Mrs Tesman? Oh, Thea!

**Mrs Elvsted**   I'm sorry, I'll try to remember. Yes – if you had any idea –

**Hedda** (*casually*)   Eilert Loevborg's been up there, too, for about three years, hasn't he?

**Mrs Elvsted** (*looks at her uncertainly*)  Eilert Loevborg? Yes,
he has.

**Hedda**  Did you know him before? When you were here?

**Mrs Elvsted**  No, not really. That is – I knew him by
name, of course.

**Hedda**  But up there, he used to visit you?

**Mrs Elvsted**  Yes, he used to come and see us every
day. To give the children lessons. I found I couldn't do
that as well as manage the house.

**Hedda**  I'm sure you couldn't. And your husband – ? I
suppose being a magistrate he has to be away from home a
good deal?

**Mrs Elvsted**  Yes. You see, Mrs – you see, Hedda, he
has to cover the whole district.

**Hedda** (*leans against the arm of* **Mrs Elvsted**'s *chair*)  Poor,
pretty little Thea! Now you must tell me the whole story.
From beginning to end.

**Mrs Elvsted**  Well – what do you want to know?

**Hedda**  What kind of a man is your husband, Thea? I
mean, as a person. Is he kind to you?

**Mrs Elvsted** (*evasively*)  I'm sure he does his best to be.

**Hedda**  I only wonder if he isn't too old for you. There's
more than twenty years between you, isn't there?

**Mrs Elvsted** (*irritably*)  Yes, there's that, too. Oh, there
are so many things. We're different in every way. We've
nothing in common. Nothing whatever.

**Hedda**  But he loves you, surely? In his own way?

**Mrs Elvsted**  Oh, I don't know. I think he finds me
useful. And then I don't cost much to keep. I'm cheap.

**Hedda**  Now you're being stupid.

**Mrs Elvsted** (*shakes her head*)  It can't be any different.

With him. He doesn't love anyone except himself. And perhaps the children – a little.

**Hedda** He must be fond of Eilert Loevborg, Thea.

**Mrs Elvsted** (*looks at her*) Eilert Loevborg? What makes you think that?

**Hedda** Well, if he sends you all the way down here to look for him – (*Smiles almost imperceptibly.*) Besides, you said so yourself to Tesman.

**Mrs Elvsted** (*with a nervous twitch*) Did I? Oh yes, I suppose I did. (*Impulsively, but keeping her voice low.*) Well, I might as well tell you the whole story. It's bound to come out sooner or later.

**Hedda** But, my dear Thea – ?

**Mrs Elvsted** My husband had no idea I was coming here.

**Hedda** What? Your husband didn't know?

**Mrs Elvsted** No, of course not. As a matter of fact, he wasn't even there. He was away at the assizes. Oh, I couldn't stand it any longer, Hedda! I just couldn't. I'd be so dreadfully lonely up there now.

**Hedda** Go on.

**Mrs Elvsted** So I packed a few things. Secretly. And went.

**Hedda** Without telling anyone?

**Mrs Elvsted** Yes. I caught the train and came straight here.

**Hedda** But, my dear Thea! How brave of you!

**Mrs Elvsted** (*gets up and walks across the room*) Well, what else could I do?

**Hedda** But what do you suppose your husband will say when you get back?

**Mrs Elvsted** (*by the table, looks at her*)  Back there? To him?

**Hedda**  Yes. Surely – ?

**Mrs Elvsted**  I shall never go back to him.

**Hedda** (*gets up and goes closer*)  You mean you've left your home for good?

**Mrs Elvsted**  Yes. I didn't see what else I could do.

**Hedda**  But to do it so openly!

**Mrs Elvsted**  Oh, it's no use trying to keep a thing like that secret.

**Hedda**  But what do you suppose people will say?

**Mrs Elvsted**  They can say what they like. (*Sits sadly, wearily on the sofa.*) I had to do it.

**Hedda** (*after a short silence*)  What do you intend to do now? How are you going to live?

**Mrs Elvsted**  I don't know. I only know that I must live wherever Eilert Loevborg is. If I am to go on living.

**Hedda** (*moves a chair from the table, sits on it near* **Mrs Elvsted** *and strokes her hands*)  Tell me, Thea, how did this – friendship between you and Eilert Loevborg begin?

**Mrs Elvsted**  Oh, it came about gradually. I developed a kind of – power over him.

**Hedda**  Oh?

**Mrs Elvsted**  He gave up his old habits. Not because I asked him to. I'd never have dared to do that. I suppose he just noticed I didn't like that kind of thing. So he gave it up.

**Hedda** (*hides a smile*)  So you've made a new man of him! Clever little Thea!

**Mrs Elvsted**  Yes – anyway, he says I have. And he's made a – sort of – real person of me. Taught me to think

– and to understand all kinds of things.

**Hedda**   Did he give you lessons, too?

**Mrs Elvsted**   Not exactly lessons. But he talked to me. About – oh, you've no idea – so many things! And then he let me work with him. Oh, it was wonderful. I was so happy to be allowed to help him.

**Hedda**   Did he allow you to help him?

**Mrs Elvsted**   Yes. Whenever he wrote anything we always – did it together.

**Hedda**   Like good friends?

**Mrs Elvsted** (*eagerly*)   Friends! Yes – why, Hedda, that's exactly the word he used! Oh, I ought to feel so happy. But I can't. I don't know if it will last.

**Hedda**   You don't seem very sure of him.

**Mrs Elvsted** (*sadly*)   Something stands between Eilert Loevborg and me. The shadow of another woman.

**Hedda**   Who can that be?

**Mrs Elvsted**   I don't know. Someone he used to be friendly with in – in the old days. Someone he's never been able to forget.

**Hedda**   What has he told you about her?

**Mrs Elvsted**   Oh, he only mentioned her once, casually.

**Hedda**   Well! What did he say?

**Mrs Elvsted**   He said when he left her she tried to shoot him with a pistol.

**Hedda** (*cold, controlled*)   What nonsense. People don't do such things. The kind of people we know.

**Mrs Elvsted**   No. I think it must have been that red-haired singer he used to –

**Hedda**   Ah yes, very probably.

**Mrs Elvsted**    I remember they used to say she always carried a loaded pistol.

**Hedda**    Well then, it must be her.

**Mrs Elvsted**    But, Hedda, I hear she's come back, and is living here. Oh, I'm so desperate – !

**Hedda** (*glances towards the rear room*)    Ssh! Tesman's coming. (*Gets up and whispers.*) Thea, we mustn't breathe a word about this to anyone.

**Mrs Elvsted** (*jumps up*)    Oh, no, no! Please don't!

**George Tesman** *appears from the right in the rear room with a letter in his hand, and comes into the drawing-room.*

**Tesman**    Well, here's my little epistle all signed and sealed.

**Hedda**    Good. I think Mrs Elvsted wants to go now. Wait a moment – I'll see you as far as the garden gate.

**Tesman**    Er – Hedda, do you think Bertha could deal with this?

**Hedda** (*takes the letter*)    I'll give her instructions.

**Bertha** *enters from the hall.*

**Bertha**    Judge Brack is here and asks if he may pay his respects to madam and the Doctor.

**Hedda**    Yes, ask him to be so good as to come in. And – wait a moment – drop this letter in the post box.

**Bertha** (*takes the letter*)    Very good, madam.

*She opens the door for* **Judge Brack**, *and goes out.* **Judge Brack** *is forty-five; rather short, but well built, and elastic in his movements. He has a roundish face with an aristocratic profile. His hair, cut short, is still almost black, and is carefully barbered. Eyes lively and humorous. Thick eyebrows. His moustache is also thick, and is trimmed square at the ends. He is wearing outdoor clothes which are elegant but a little too youthful for him. He has a monocle in one eye; now and then he lets it drop.*

**Brack** (*hat in hand, bows*)   May one presume to call so early?

**Hedda**   One may presume.

**Tesman** (*shakes his hand*)   You're welcome here any time. Judge Brack – Mrs Rysing.

**Hedda** *sighs.* (name)

**Brack** (*bows*)   Ah – charmed –

**Hedda** (*looks at him and laughs*)   What fun to be able to see you by daylight for once, Judge.

**Brack**   Do I look – different?

**Hedda**   Yes. A little younger, I think.

**Brack**   Too kind.

**Tesman**   Well, what do you think of Hedda? What? Doesn't she look well? Hasn't she filled out – ?

**Hedda**   Oh, do stop it. You ought to be thanking Judge Brack for all the inconvenience he's put himself to –

**Brack**   Nonsense, it was a pleasure –

**Hedda**   You're a loyal friend. But my other friend is pining to get away. Au revoir, Judge. I won't be a minute.

*Mutual salutations.* **Mrs Elvsted** *and* **Hedda** *go out through the hall.*

**Brack**   Well, is your wife satisfied with everything?

**Tesman**   Yes, we can't thank you enough. That is – we may have to shift one or two things around, she tells me. And we're short of one or two little items we'll have to purchase.

**Brack**   Oh? Really?

**Tesman**   But you mustn't worry your head about that. Hedda says she'll get what's needed. I say, why don't we sit down? What?

**Brack**   Thanks, just for a moment. (*Sits at the table.*)
There's something I'd like to talk to you about, my dear
Tesman.

**Tesman**   Oh? Ah yes, of course. (*Sits.*) After the feast
comes the reckoning. What?

**Brack**   Oh, never mind about the financial side – there's
no hurry about that. Though I could wish we'd arranged
things a little less palatially.

*[like a palace]*

**Tesman**   Good heavens, that'd never have done. Think
of Hedda, my dear chap. You know her. I couldn't possibly
ask her to live like a petty bourgeois.

**Brack**   No, no – that's just the problem.

**Tesman**   Anyway, it can't be long now before my
nomination comes through.

**Brack**   Well, you know, these things often take time.

**Tesman**   Have you heard any more news? What?

**Brack**   Nothing definite. (*Changing the subject.*) Oh, by the
way, I have one piece of news for you.

**Tesman**   What?

**Brack**   Your old friend Eilert Loevborg is back in town.

**Tesman**   I know that already.

**Brack**   Oh? How did you hear that?

**Tesman**   She told me. That lady who went out with
Hedda.

**Brack**   I see. What was her name? I didn't catch it.

**Tesman**   Mrs Elvsted.

**Brack**   Oh, the magistrate's wife. Yes, Loevborg's been
living up near them, hasn't he?

**Tesman**   I'm delighted to hear he's become a decent
human being again.

**Brack**  Yes, so they say.

**Tesman**  I gather he's published a new book, too. What?

**Brack**  Indeed he has.

**Tesman**  I hear it's created rather a stir.

**Brack**  Quite an unusual stir.

**Tesman**  I say, isn't that splendid news! He's such a gifted chap – and I was afraid he'd gone to the dogs for good.

**Brack**  Most people thought he had.

**Tesman**  But I can't think what he'll do now. How on earth will he manage to make ends meet? What?

*As he speaks his last words* **Hedda** *enters from the hall.*

**Hedda** (*to* **Brack**, *laughs slightly scornfully*)  Tesman is always worrying about making ends meet.

**Tesman**  We were talking about poor Eilert Loevborg, Hedda dear.

**Hedda** (*gives him a quick look*)  Oh, were you? (*Sits in the armchair by the stove and asks casually.*) Is he in trouble?

**Tesman**  Well, he must have run through his inheritance long ago by now. And he can't write a new book every year. What? So I'm wondering what's going to become of him.

**Brack**  I may be able to enlighten you there.

**Tesman**  Oh?

**Brack**  You mustn't forget he has relatives who wield a good deal of influence.

**Tesman**  Relatives? Oh, they've quite washed their hands of him, I'm afraid.

**Brack**  They used to regard him as the hope of the family.

**Tesman**  Used to, yes. But he's put an end to that.

**Hedda**  Who knows? (*With a little smile.*) I hear the Elvsteds have made a new man of him.

**Brack**  And then this book he's just published –

**Tesman**  Well, let's hope they find something for him. I've just written him a note. Oh, by the way, Hedda, I asked him to come over and see us this evening.

**Brack**  But, my dear chap, you're coming to me this evening. My bachelor party. You promised me last night when I met you at the boat.

**Hedda**  Had you forgotten, Tesman?

**Tesman**  Good heavens, yes, I'd quite forgotten.

**Brack**  Anyway, you can be quite sure he won't turn up here.

**Tesman**  Why do you think that? What?

**Brack** (*a little unwillingly, gets up and rests his hands on the back of his chair*)  My dear Tesman – and you, too, Mrs Tesman – there's something I feel you ought to know.

**Tesman**  Concerning Eilert –

**Brack**  Concerning him and you.

**Tesman**  Well, my dear Judge, tell us, please!

**Brack**  You must be prepared for your nomination not to come through quite as quickly as you hope and expect.

**Tesman** (*jumps up uneasily*)  Is anything wrong? What?

**Brack**  There's a possibility that the appointment may be decided by competition –

**Tesman**  Competition! Hedda, fancy that!

**Hedda** (*leans further back in her chair*)  Ah! How interesting!

**Tesman**  But who else –? I say, you don't mean –?

**Brack**  Exactly. By competition with Eilert Loevborg.

**Tesman** (*clasps his hands in alarm*)   No, no, but this is inconceivable! It's absolutely impossible! What?

**Brack**   Hm. We may find it'll happen, all the same.

**Tesman**   No, but – Judge Brack, they couldn't be so inconsiderate towards me! (*Waves his arms.*) I mean, by Jove, I – I'm a married man! It was on the strength of this that Hedda and I *got* married! We've run up some pretty hefty debts. And borrowed money from Auntie Juju! I mean, good heavens, they practically promised me the appointment. What?

**Brack**   Well, well, I'm sure you'll get it. But you'll have to go through a competition.

**Hedda** (*motionless in her armchair*)   How exciting, Tesman. It'll be a kind of duel, by Jove.

**Tesman**   My dear Hedda, how can you take it so lightly?

**Hedda** (*as before*)   I'm not. I can't wait to see who's going to win.

**Brack**   In any case, Mrs Tesman, it's best you should know how things stand. I mean before you commit yourself to these little items I hear you're threatening to purchase.

**Hedda**   I can't allow this to alter my plans.

**Brack**   Indeed? Well, that's your business. Goodbye. (*To* **Tesman**.) I'll come and collect you on the way home from my afternoon walk.

**Tesman**   Oh, yes, yes. I'm sorry, I'm all upside down just now.

**Hedda** (*lying in her chair, holds out her hand*)   Goodbye, Judge. See you this afternoon.

**Brack**   Thank you. Goodbye, goodbye.

**Tesman** (*sees him to the door*)   Goodbye, my dear Judge. You will excuse me, won't you?

**Judge Brack** *goes out through the hall.*

**Tesman** (*pacing up and down*)   Oh, Hedda! One oughtn't to go plunging off on wild adventures. What?

**Hedda** (*looks at him and smiles*)   Like you're doing?

**Tesman**   Yes. I mean, there's no denying it, it was a pretty big adventure to go off and get married and set up house merely on expectation.

**Hedda**   Perhaps you're right.

**Tesman**   Well, anyway, we have our home, Hedda. My word, yes! The home we dreamed of. And set our hearts on. What?

**Hedda** (*gets up slowly, wearily*)   You agreed that we should enter society. And keep open house. That was the bargain.

**Tesman**   Yes. Good heavens, I was looking forward to it all so much. To seeing you play hostess to a select circle! By Jove! What? Ah, well, for the time being we shall have to make do with each other's company, Hedda. Perhaps have Auntie Juju in now and then. Oh dear, this wasn't at all what you had in mind –

**Hedda**   I won't be able to have a liveried footman. For a start.

**Tesman**   Oh no, we couldn't possibly afford a footman.

**Hedda**   And the bay mare you promised me –

**Tesman** (*fearfully*)   Bay mare!

**Hedda**   I mustn't even think of that now.

**Tesman**   Heaven forbid!

**Hedda** (*walks across the room*)   Ah, well. I still have one thing left to amuse myself with.

**Tesman** (*joyfully*)   Thank goodness for that. What's that, Hedda? What?

**Hedda** (*in the open doorway, looks at him with concealed scorn*) My pistols, George darling.

**Tesman** (*alarmed*)   Pistols!

**Hedda** (*her eyes cold*)   General Gabler's pistols.

*She goes into the rear room and disappears.*

**Tesman** (*runs to the doorway and calls after her*)   For heaven's sake, Hedda dear, don't touch those things. They're dangerous. Hedda – please – for my sake! What?

# Act Two

*The same as in Act One, except that the piano has been removed and an elegant little writing-table, with a bookcase, stands in its place. By the sofa on the left a smaller table has been placed. Most of the flowers have been removed.* **Mrs Elvsted**'s *bouquet stands on the larger table, downstage. It is afternoon.*

**Hedda**, *dressed to receive callers, is alone in the room. She is standing by the open french windows, loading a revolver. The pair to it is lying in an open pistol-case on the writing-table.*

**Hedda** (*looks down into the garden and calls*)   Good afternoon, Judge.

**Brack** (*in the distance, below*)   Afternoon, Mrs Tesman.

**Hedda** (*raises the pistol and takes aim*)   I'm going to shoot you, Judge Brack.

**Brack** (*shouts from below*)   No, no, no! Don't aim that thing at me!

**Hedda**   This'll teach you to enter houses by the back door.

*She fires.*

**Brack** (*below*)   Have you gone completely out of your mind?

**Hedda**   Oh dear! Did I hit you?

**Brack** (*still outside*)   Stop playing these silly tricks.

**Hedda**   All right, Judge. Come along in.

**Judge Brack**, *dressed for a bachelor party, enters through the french windows. He has a light overcoat on his arm.*

**Brack**   For God's sake, haven't you stopped fooling around with those things yet? What are you trying to hit?

**Hedda**   Oh, I was just shooting at the sky.

**Brack** (*takes the pistol gently from her hand*)   By your leave, ma'am. (*Looks at it.*) Ah, yes – I know this old friend well. (*Looks around.*) Where's the case? Oh, yes. (*Puts the pistol in the case and closes it.*) That's enough of that little game for today.

**Hedda**   Well, what on earth *am* I to do?

**Brack**   You haven't had any visitors?

**Hedda** (*closes the french windows*)   Not one. I suppose the best people are all still in the country.

**Brack**   Your husband isn't home yet?

**Hedda** (*locks the pistol-case away in a drawer of the writing-table*) No. The moment he'd finished eating he ran off to his aunties. He wasn't expecting you so early.

**Brack**   Ah, why didn't I think of that? How stupid of me.

**Hedda** (*turns her head and looks at him*)   Why stupid?

**Brack**   I'd have come a little sooner.

**Hedda** (*walks across the room*)   There'd have been no one to receive you. I've been in my room since lunch, dressing.

**Brack**   You haven't a tiny crack in the door through which we might have negotiated?

**Hedda**   You forgot to arrange one.

**Brack**   Another stupidity.

**Hedda**   Well, we'll have to sit down here. And wait. Tesman won't be back for some time.

**Brack**   Sad. Well, I'll be patient.

**Hedda** *sits on the corner of the sofa.* **Brack** *puts his coat over the back of the nearest chair and seats himself, keeping his hat in his hand. Short pause. They look at each other.*

**Hedda**   Well?

**Brack** (*in the same tone of voice*)   Well?

**Hedda**   I asked first.

**Brack** (*leans forward slightly*)  Yes, well, now we can enjoy a nice, cosy little chat – Mrs Hedda.

**Hedda** (*leans further back in her chair*)  It seems ages since we had a talk. I don't count last night or this morning.

**Brack**  You mean: *à deux*?

**Hedda**  Mm – yes. That's roughly what I meant.

**Brack**  I've been longing so much for you to come home.

**Hedda**  So have I.

**Brack**  You? Really, Mrs Hedda? And I thought you were having such a wonderful honeymoon.

**Hedda**  Oh, yes. Wonderful!

**Brack**  But your husband wrote such ecstatic letters.

**Hedda**  He! Oh, yes! He thinks life has nothing better to offer than rooting around in libraries and copying old pieces of parchment, or whatever it is he does.

**Brack** (*a little maliciously*)  Well, that *is* his life. Most of it, anyway.

**Hedda**  Yes, I know. Well, it's all right for him. But for me! Oh no, my dear Judge. I've been bored to death.

**Brack** (*sympathetically*)  Do you mean that? Seriously?

**Hedda**  Yes. Can you imagine? Six whole months without ever meeting a single person who was one of us, and to whom I could talk about the kind of things we talk about.

**Brack**  Yes, I can understand. I'd miss that, too.

**Hedda**  That wasn't the worst, though.

**Brack**  What was?

**Hedda**  Having to spend every minute of one's life with – with the same person.

**Brack** (*nods*)  Yes. What a thought! Morning; noon; *and* –

**Hedda** (*coldly*)  As I said: every minute of one's life.

**Brack**   I stand corrected. But dear Tesman is such a clever fellow, I should have thought one ought to be able –

**Hedda**   Tesman is only interested in one thing, my dear Judge. His special subject.

**Brack**   True.

**Hedda**   And people who are only interested in one thing doesn't make the most amusing company. Not for long, anyway.

**Brack**   Not even when they happen to be the person one loves?

**Hedda**   Oh, don't use that sickly, stupid word.

**Brack** (*starts*)   But, Mrs Hedda –!

**Hedda** (*half laughing, half annoyed*)   You just try it, Judge. Listening to the history of civilization morning, noon and –

**Brack** (*corrects her*)   Every minute of one's life.

**Hedda**   All right. Oh, and those domestic industries of Brabant in the Middle Ages! That really is beyond the limit.

**Brack** (*looks at her searchingly*)   But, tell me – if you feel like this why on earth did you –? Hm –

**Hedda**   Why on earth did I marry George Tesman?

**Brack**   If you like to put it that way.

**Hedda**   Do you think it so very strange?

**Brack**   Yes – and no, Mrs Hedda.

**Hedda**   I'd danced myself tired, Judge. I felt my time was up – (*Gives a slight shudder.*) No, I mustn't say that. Or even think it.

**Brack**   You've no rational cause to think it.

**Hedda**   Oh – cause, cause – (*Looks searchingly at him.*) After all, George Tesman – well, I mean, he's a very respectable man.

**Brack**   Very respectable, sound as a rock. No denying that.

**Hedda**   And there's nothing exactly ridiculous about him. Is there?

**Brack**   Ridiculous? N-no, I wouldn't say that.

**Hedda**   Mm. He's very clever at collecting material and all that, isn't he? I mean, he may go quite far in time.

**Brack** (*looks at her a little uncertainly*)   I thought you believed, like everyone else, that he would become a very prominent man.

**Hedda** (*looks tired*)   Yes, I did. And when he came and begged me on his bended knees to be allowed to love and to cherish me, I didn't see why I shouldn't let him.

**Brack**   No, well – if one looks at it like that –

**Hedda**   It was more than my other admirers were prepared to do, Judge dear.

**Brack** (*laughs*)   Well, I can't answer for the others. As far as I myself am concerned, you know I've always had a considerable respect for the institution of marriage. As an institution.

**Hedda** (*lightly*)   Oh, I've never entertained any hopes of you.

**Brack**   All I want is to have a circle of friends whom I can trust, whom I can help with advice or – or by any other means, and into whose houses I may come and go as a – trusted friend.

**Hedda**   Of the husband?

**Brack** (*bows*)   Preferably, to be frank, of the wife. And of the husband too, of course. Yes, you know, this kind of triangle is a delightful arrangement for all parties concerned.

**Hedda**   Yes, I often longed for a third person while I was away. Oh, those hours we spent alone in railway

compartments –

**Brack**   Fortunately your honeymoon is now over.

**Hedda** (*shakes her head*)   There's a long, long way still to go. I've only reached a stop on the line.

**Brack**   Why not jump out and stretch your legs a little, Mrs Hedda?

**Hedda**   I'm not the jumping sort.

**Brack**   Aren't you?

**Hedda**   No. There's always someone around who –

**Brack** (*laughs*)   Who looks at one's legs?

**Hedda**   Yes. Exactly.

**Brack**   Well, but surely –

**Hedda** (*with a gesture of rejection*)   I don't like it. I'd rather stay where I am. Sitting in the compartment. *À deux*.

**Brack**   But suppose a third person were to step into the compartment?

**Hedda**   That would be different.

**Brack**   A trusted friend – someone who understood –

**Hedda**   And was lively and amusing –

**Brack**   And interested in – more subjects than one –

**Hedda** (*sighs audibly*)   Yes, that'd be a relief.

**Brack** (*hears the front door open and shut*)   The triangle is completed.

**Hedda** (*half under her breath*)   And the train goes on.

**George Tesman**, *in grey walking dress with a soft felt hat, enters from the hall. He has a number of paper-covered books under his arm and in his pockets.*

**Tesman** (*goes over to the table by the corner sofa*)   Phew! It's too hot to be lugging all this around. (*Puts the books down.*)

I'm positively sweating, Hedda. Why, hullo, hullo! You here already, Judge? What? Bertha didn't tell me.

**Brack** (*gets up*)  I came in through the garden.

**Hedda**  What are all those books you've got there?

**Tesman** (*stands glancing through them*)  Oh, some new publications dealing with my special subject. I had to buy them.

**Hedda**  Your special subject?

**Brack**  His special subject, Mrs Tesman.

**Brack** *and* **Hedda** *exchange a smile.*

**Hedda**  Haven't you collected enough material on your special subject?

**Tesman**  My dear Hedda, one can never have too much. One must keep abreast of what other people are writing.

**Hedda**  Yes. Of course.

**Tesman** (*rooting among the books*)  Look – I bought a copy of Eilert Loevborg's new book, too. (*Holds it out to her.*) Perhaps you'd like to have a look at it, Hedda? What?

**Hedda**  No, thank you. Er – yes, perhaps I will, later.

**Tesman**  I glanced through it on my way home.

**Brack**  What's your opinion – as a specialist on the subject?

**Tesman**  I'm amazed how sound and balanced it is. He never used to write like that. (*Gathers his books together.*) Well, I must get down to these at once. I can hardly wait to cut the pages. Oh, I've got to change, too. (*To* **Brack**,) We don't have to be off just yet, do we? What?

**Brack**  Heavens, no. We've plenty of time yet.

**Tesman**  Good, I needn't hurry, then. (*Goes with his books, but stops and turns in the doorway.*) Oh, by the way, Hedda, Auntie Juju won't be coming to see you this evening.

**Hedda**   Won't she? Oh – the hat, I suppose.

**Tesman**   Good heavens, no. How could you think such a thing of Auntie Juju? Fancy –! No, Auntie Rena's very ill.

**Hedda**   She always is.

**Tesman**   Yes, but today she's been taken really bad.

**Hedda**   Oh, then it's quite understandable that the other one should want to stay with her. Well, I shall have to swallow my disappointment.

**Tesman**   You can't imagine how happy Auntie Juju was in spite of everything. At your looking so well after the honeymoon!

**Hedda** (*half beneath her breath, as she rises*)   Oh, these everlasting aunts!

**Tesman**   What?

**Hedda** (*goes over to the french windows*)   Nothing.

**Tesman**   Oh. All right. (*Goes into the rear room and out of sight.*)

**Brack**   What was that about the hat?

**Hedda**   Oh, something that happened with Miss Tesman this morning. She'd put her hat down on a chair. (*Looks at him and smiles.*) And I pretended to think it was the servant's.

**Brack** (*shakes his head*)   But, my dear Mrs Hedda, how could you do such a thing? To that poor old lady?

**Hedda** (*nervously, walking across the room*)   Sometimes a mood like that hits me. And I can't stop myself. (*Throws herself down in the armchair by the stove.*) Oh, I don't know how to explain it.

**Brack** (*behind her chair*)   You're not really happy. That's the answer.

**Hedda** (*stares ahead of her*)   Why on earth should I be happy? Can you give me a reason?

**Brack**  Yes. For one thing you've got the home you always wanted.

**Hedda** (*looks at him*)  You really believe that story?

**Brack**  You mean it isn't true?

**Hedda**  Oh, yes, it's partly true.

**Brack**  Well?

**Hedda**  It's true I got Tesman to see me home from parties last summer –

**Brack**  It was a pity my home lay in another direction.

**Hedda**  Yes. Your interests lay in another direction, too.

**Brack** (*laughs*)  That's naughty of you, Mrs Hedda. But to return to you and George –

**Hedda**  Well, we walked past this house one evening. And poor Tesman was fidgeting in his boots trying to find something to talk about. I felt sorry for the great scholar –

**Brack** (*smiles incredulously*)  Did you? Hm.

**Hedda**  Yes, honestly I did. Well, to help him out of his misery, I happened to say quite frivolously how much I'd love to live in this house.

**Brack**  Was that all?

**Hedda**  That evening, yes.

**Brack**  But – afterwards?

**Hedda**  Yes. My little frivolity had its consequences, my dear Judge.

**Brack**  Our little frivolities do. Much too often, unfortunately.

**Hedda**  Thank you. Well, it was our mutual admiration for the late Prime Minister's house that brought George Tesman and me together on common ground. So we got engaged, and we got married, and we went on our honeymoon, and – Ah well, Judge, I've – made my bed

and I must lie in it, I was about to say.

**Brack**   How utterly fantastic! And you didn't really care in the least about the house?

**Hedda**   God knows I didn't.

**Brack**   Yes, but now that we've furnished it so beautifully for you?

**Hedda**   Ugh – all the rooms smell of lavender and dried roses. But perhaps Auntie Juju brought that in.

**Brack** (*laughs*)   More likely the Prime Minister's widow, rest her soul.

**Hedda**   Yes, it's got the odour of death about it. It reminds me of the flowers one has worn at a ball – the morning after. (*Clasps her hands behind her neck, leans back in the chair and looks up at him.*) Oh, my dear Judge, you've no idea how hideously bored I'm going to be out here.

**Brack**   Couldn't you find some – occupation, Mrs Hedda? Like your husband?

**Hedda**   Occupation? That'd interest me?

**Brack**   Well – preferably.

**Hedda**   God knows what. I've often thought – (*Breaks off.*) No, that wouldn't work either.

**Brack**   Who knows? Tell me about it.

**Hedda**   I was thinking – if I could persuade Tesman to go into politics, for example.

**Brack** (*laughs*)   Tesman! No, honestly, I don't think he's quite cut out to be a politician.

**Hedda**   Perhaps not. But if I could persuade him to have a go at it?

**Brack**   What satisfaction would that give you? If he turned out to be no good? Why do you want to make him do that?

**Hedda**    Because I'm bored. (*After a moment.*) You feel
there's absolutely no possibility of Tesman becoming Prime
Minister, then?

**Brack**    Well, you know, Mrs Hedda, for one thing he'd
have to be pretty well off before he could become that.

**Hedda** (*gets up impatiently*)    There you are! (*Walks across the
room.*) It's this wretched poverty that makes life so hateful.
And ludicrous. Well, it is!

**Brack**    I don't think that's the real cause.

**Hedda**    What is, then?

**Brack**    Nothing really exciting has ever happened to you.

**Hedda**    Nothing serious, you mean?

**Brack**    Call it that if you like. But now perhaps it may.

**Hedda** (*tosses her head*)    Oh, you're thinking of this
competition for that wretched professorship? That's
Tesman's affair. I'm not going to waste my time worrying
about that.

**Brack**    Very well, let's forget about that, then. But
suppose you were to find yourself faced with what people
call – to use the conventional phrase – the most solemn of
human responsibilities? (*Smiles.*) A new responsibility, little
Mrs Hedda.

**Hedda** (*angrily*)    Be quiet! Nothing like that's going to
happen.

**Brack** (*warily*)    We'll talk about it again in a year's time.
If not earlier.

**Hedda** (*curtly*)    I've no leanings in that direction, Judge. I
don't want any – responsibilities.

**Brack**    But surely you must feel some inclination to make
use of that – natural talent every woman –

**Hedda** (*over by the french windows*)    Oh, be quiet, I say! I
often think there's only one thing for which I have any

natural talent.

**Brack** (*goes closer*)   And what is that, if I may be so bold as to ask?

**Hedda** (*stands looking out*)   For boring myself to death. Now you know. (*Turns, looks towards the rear room and laughs.*) Talking of boring, here comes the professor.

**Brack** (*quietly, warningly*)   Now, now, now, Mrs Hedda!

**George Tesman**, *in evening dress, with gloves and hat in his hand, enters through the rear room from the right.*

**Tesman**   Hedda, hasn't any message come from Eilert? What?

**Hedda**   No.

**Tesman**   Ah, then we'll have him here presently. You wait and see.

**Brack**   You really think he'll come?

**Tesman**   Yes, I'm almost sure he will. What you were saying about him this morning is just gossip.

**Brack**   Oh?

**Tesman**   Yes. Auntie Juju said she didn't believe he'd ever dare to stand in my way again. Fancy that!

**Brack**   Then everything in the garden's lovely.

**Tesman** (*puts his hat, with his gloves in it, on a chair, right*) Yes, but you really must let me wait for him as long as possible.

**Brack**   We've plenty of time. No one'll be turning up at my place before seven or half past.

**Tesman**   Ah, then we can keep Hedda company a little longer. And see if he turns up. What?

**Hedda** (*picks up* **Brack**'s *coat and hat and carries them over to the corner sofa*)   And if the worst comes to the worst, Mr Loevborg can sit here and talk to me.

**Brack** (*offering to take his things from her*)   No, please. What do you mean by 'if the worst comes to the worst'?

**Hedda**   If he doesn't want to go with you and Tesman.

**Tesman** (*looks doubtfully at her*)   I say, Hedda, do you think it'll be all right for him to stay here with you? What? Remember Auntie Juju isn't coming.

**Hedda**   Yes, but Mrs Elvsted is. The three of us can have a cup of tea together.

**Tesman**   Ah, that'll be all right.

**Brack** (*smiles*)   It's probably the safest solution as far as he's concerned.

**Hedda**   Why?

**Brack**   My dear Mrs Tesman, you always say of my little bachelor parties that they should only be attended by men of the strongest principles.

**Hedda**   But Mr Loevborg is a man of principle now. You know what they say about a reformed sinner –

**Bertha** *enters from the hall.*

**Bertha**   Madam, there's a gentleman here who wants to see you –

**Hedda**   Ask him to come in.

**Tesman** (*quietly*)   I'm sure it's him. By Jove. Fancy that!

**Eilert Loevborg** *enters from the hall. He is slim and lean, of the same age as* **Tesman**, *but looks older and somewhat haggard. His hair and beard are of a blackish-brown; his face is long and pale, but with a couple of reddish patches on his cheekbones. He is dressed in an elegant and fairly new black suit, and carries black gloves and a top-hat in his hand. He stops just inside the door and bows abruptly. He seems somewhat embarrassed.*

**Tesman** (*goes over and shakes his hand*)   My dear Eilert! How grand to see you again after all these years!

**Loevborg** (*speaks softly*)   It was good of you to write,

George. (*Goes nearer to* **Hedda**.) May I shake hands with you, too, Mrs Tesman?

**Hedda** (*accepts his hand*)   Delighted to see you, Mr Loevborg. (*With a gesture.*) I don't know if you two gentlemen –

**Loevborg** (*bows slightly*)   Judge Brack, I believe.

**Brack** (*also with a slight bow*)   Correct. We – met some years ago –

**Tesman** (*puts his hands on* **Loevborg**'s *shoulders*)   Now, you're to treat this house just as though it were your own home, Eilert. Isn't that right, Hedda? I hear you've decided to settle here again. What?

**Loevborg**   Yes, I have.

**Tesman**   Quite understandable. Oh, by the by – I've just bought your new book. Though to tell the truth I haven't found time to read it yet.

**Loevborg**   You needn't bother.

**Tesman**   Oh? Why?

**Loevborg**   There's nothing much in it.

**Tesman**   By Jove, fancy hearing that from you!

**Brack**   But everyone's praising it.

**Loevborg**   That was exactly what I wanted to happen. So I only wrote what I knew everyone would agree with.

**Brack**   Very sensible.

**Tesman**   Yes, but my dear Eilert –

**Loevborg**   I want to try to re-establish myself. To begin again – from the beginning.

**Tesman** (*a little embarrassed*)   Yes, I – er – suppose you do. What?

**Loevborg** (*smiles, puts down his hat and takes a package wrapped in paper from his coat pocket*)   But when this gets published –

George Tesman – read it. This is my real book. The one
in which I have spoken with my own voice.

**Tesman**   Oh, really? What's it about?

**Loevborg**   It's the sequel.

**Tesman**   Sequel? To what?

**Loevborg**   To the other book.

**Tesman**   The one that's just come out?

**Loevborg**   Yes.

**Tesman**   But my dear Eilert, that covers the subject right
up to the present day.

**Loevborg**   It does. But this is about the future.

**Tesman**   The future! But, I say, we don't know anything
about that.

**Loevborg**   No. But there are one or two things that need
to be said about it. (*Opens the package.*) Here, have a look.

**Tesman**   Surely that's not your handwriting?

**Loevborg**   I dictated it. (*Turns the pages.*) It's in two parts.
The first deals with the forces that will shape our
civilization. (*Turns further on towards the end.*) And the second
indicates the direction in which that civilization may
develop.

**Tesman**   Amazing! I'd never think of writing about
anything like that.

**Hedda** (*by the french windows, drumming on the pane*)   No. You
wouldn't.

**Loevborg** (*puts the pages back into their cover and lays the
package on the table*)   I brought it because I thought I might
possibly read you a few pages this evening.

**Tesman**   I say, what a kind idea! Oh, but this evening – ?
(*Glances at* **Brack**.) I'm not quite sure whether –

**Loevborg**   Well, some other time, then. There's no hurry.

**Brack**   The truth is, Mr Loevborg, I'm giving a little dinner this evening. In Tesman's honour, you know.

**Loevborg** (*looks round for his hat*)   Oh – then I mustn't –

**Brack**   No, wait a minute. Won't you do me the honour of joining us?

**Loevborg** (*curtly, with decision*)   No, I can't. Thank you so much.

**Brack**   Oh, nonsense. Do – please. There'll only be a few of us. And I can promise you we shall have some good sport, as Hed – as Mrs Tesman puts it.

**Loevborg**   I've no doubt. Nevertheless.

**Brack**   You could bring your manuscript along and read it to Tesman at my place. I could lend you a room.

**Tesman**   Well, yes, that's an idea. What?

**Hedda** (*interposes*)   But, Tesman, Mr Loevborg doesn't want to go. I'm sure Mr Loevborg would much rather sit here and have supper with me.

**Loevborg** (*looks at her*)   With you, Mrs Tesman?

**Hedda**   And Mrs Elvsted.

**Loevborg**   Oh. (*Casually.*) I ran into her this afternoon.

**Hedda**   Did you? Well, she's coming here this evening. So you really must stay, Mr Loevborg. Otherwise she'll have no one to see her home.

**Loevborg**   That's true. Well – thank you, Mrs Tesman, I'll stay then.

**Hedda**   I'll just tell the servant.

*She goes to the door which leads into the hall, and rings.* **Bertha** *enters.* **Hedda** *talks softly to her and points towards the rear room.* **Bertha** *nods and goes out.*

**Tesman** (*to* **Loevborg**, *as* **Hedda** *does this*)   I say, Eilert. This new subject of yours – the – er – future – is that the

one you're going to lecture about?

**Loevborg** Yes.

**Tesman** They told me down at the bookshop that you're going to hold a series of lectures here during the autumn.

**Loevborg** Yes, I am. I – hope you don't mind, Tesman.

**Tesman** Good heavens, no! But – ?

**Loevborg** I can quite understand it might queer your pitch a little.

**Tesman** (*dejectedly*) Oh well, I can't expect you to put them off for my sake.

**Loevborg** I'll wait till your appointment's been announced.

**Tesman** You'll wait! But – but – aren't you going to compete with me for the post? What?

**Loevborg** No. I only want to defeat you in the eyes of the world.

**Tesman** Good heavens! Then Auntie Juju was right after all! Oh, I knew it, I knew it! Hear that, Hedda? Fancy! Eilert *doesn't* want to stand in our way.

**Hedda** (*curtly*) Our? Leave me out of it, please.

*She goes towards the rear room, where* **Bertha** *is setting a tray with decanters and glasses on the table.* **Hedda** *nods approval, and comes back into the drawing-room.* **Bertha** *goes out.*

**Tesman** (*while this is happening*) Judge Brack, what do you think about all this? What?

**Brack** Oh, I think honour and victory can be very splendid things –

**Tesman** Of course they can. Still –

**Hedda** (*looks at* **Tesman**, *with a cold smile*) You look as if you'd been hit by a thunderbolt.

**Tesman** Yes, I feel rather like it.

**Brack**   There was a black cloud looming up, Mrs Tesman. But it seems to have passed over.

**Hedda** (*points towards the rear room*)   Well, gentlemen, won't you go in and take a glass of cold punch?

**Brack** (*glances at his watch*)   One for the road? Yes, why not?

**Tesman**   An admirable suggestion, Hedda. Admirable! Oh, I feel so relieved!

**Hedda**   Won't you have one, too, Mr Loevborg?

**Loevborg**   No, thank you. I'd rather not.

**Brack**   Great heavens, man, cold punch isn't poison. Take my word for it.

**Loevborg**   Not for everyone, perhaps.

**Hedda**   I'll keep Mr Loevborg company while you drink.

**Tesman**   Yes, Hedda dear, would you?

*He and* **Brack** *go into the rear room, sit down, drink punch, smoke cigarettes and talk cheerfully during the following scene.* **Eilert Loevborg** *remains standing by the stove.* **Hedda** *goes to the writing-table.*

**Hedda** (*raising her voice slightly*)   I've some photographs I'd like to show you, if you'd care to see them. Tesman and I visited the Tyrol on our way home.

*She comes back with an album, places it on the table by the sofa and sits in the upstage corner of the sofa.* **Eilert Loevborg** *comes towards her, stops, and looks at her. Then he takes a chair and sits down on her left, with his back towards the rear room.*

(*Opens the album.*) You see these mountains, Mr Loevborg? That's the Ortler group. Tesman has written the name underneath. You see: 'The Ortler Group near Meran.'

**Loevborg** (*has not taken his eyes from her; says softly, slowly*)   Hedda – Gabler!

**Hedda** (*gives him a quick glance*)   Ssh!

**Loevborg** (*repeats softly*)   Hedda Gabler!

**Hedda** (*looks at the album*)   Yes, that used to be my name. When we first knew each other.

**Loevborg**   And from now on – for the rest of my life – I must teach myself never to say: Hedda Gabler.

**Hedda** (*still turning the pages*)   Yes, you must. You'd better start getting into practice. The sooner the better.

**Loevborg** (*bitterly*)   Hedda Gabler married? And to George Tesman!

**Hedda**   Yes. Well – that's life.

**Loevborg**   Oh, Hedda, Hedda! How could you throw yourself away like that?

**Hedda** (*looks sharply at him*)   Stop it.

**Loevborg**   What do you mean?

**Tesman** *comes in and goes towards the sofa.*

**Hedda** (*hears him coming and says casually*)   And this, Mr Loevborg, is the view from the Ampezzo valley. Look at these mountains. (*Glances affectionately up at* **Tesman**.) What did you say those curious mountains were called, dear?

**Tesman**   Let me have a look. Oh, those are the Dolomites.

**Hedda**   Of course. Those are the Dolomites, Mr Loevborg.

**Tesman**   Hedda, I just wanted to ask you, can't we bring some punch in here? A glass for you, anyway. What?

**Hedda**   Thank you, yes. And a biscuit or two, perhaps.

**Tesman**   You wouldn't like a cigarette?

**Hedda**   No.

**Tesman**   Right.

*He goes into the rear room and over to the right.* **Brack** *is seated*

*there, glancing occasionally at* **Hedda** *and* **Loevborg**.

**Loevborg** (*softly, as before*)  Answer me, Hedda. How could you do it?

**Hedda** (*apparently absorbed in the album*)  If you go on calling me Hedda I won't talk to you any more.

**Loevborg**  Mayn't I even when we're alone?

**Hedda**  No. You can think it. But you mustn't say it.

**Loevborg**  Oh, I see. Because you love George Tesman.

**Hedda** (*glances at him and smiles*)  Love? Don't be funny.

**Loevborg**  You don't love him?

**Hedda**  I don't intend to be unfaithful to him. That's not what I want.

**Loevborg**  Hedda – just tell me one thing –

**Hedda**  Ssh!

**Tesman** *enters from the rear room, carrying a tray.*

**Tesman**  Here we are! Here come the refreshments.

*He puts the tray down on the table.*

**Hedda**  Why didn't you ask the servant to bring it in?

**Tesman** (*fills the glasses*)  I like waiting on you, Hedda.

**Hedda**  But you've filled both glasses. Mr Loevborg doesn't want to drink.

**Tesman**  Yes, but Mrs Elvsted'll be here soon.

**Hedda**  Oh yes, that's true. Mrs Elvsted –

**Tesman**  Had you forgotten her? What?

**Hedda**  We're so absorbed with these photographs. (*Shows him one.*) You remember this little village?

**Tesman**  Oh, that one down by the Brenner Pass. We spent a night there –

**Hedda**    Yes, and met all those amusing people.

**Tesman**    Oh yes, it was there, wasn't it? By Jove, if only we could have had you with us, Eilert! Ah, well.

*He goes back into the other room and sits down with* **Brack**.

**Loevborg**    Tell me one thing, Hedda.

**Hedda**    Yes?

**Loevborg**    Didn't you love me either? Not – just a little?

**Hedda**    Well now, I wonder? No, I think we were just good friends. (*Smiles.*) You certainly poured your heart out to me.

**Loevborg**    You begged me to.

**Hedda**    Looking back on it, there was something beautiful and fascinating – and brave – about the way we told each other everything. That secret friendship no one else knew about.

**Loevborg**    Yes, Hedda, yes! Do you remember? How I used to come up to your father's house in the afternoon – and the General sat by the window and read his newspapers – with his back towards us –

**Hedda**    And we sat on the sofa in the corner –

**Loevborg**    Always reading the same illustrated magazine –

**Hedda**    We hadn't any photograph album.

**Loevborg**    Yes, Hedda. I regarded you as a kind of confessor. Told you things about myself which no one else knew about – then. Those days and nights of drinking and – oh, Hedda, what power did you have to make me confess such things?

**Hedda**    Power? You think I had some power over you?

**Loevborg**    Yes – I don't know how else to explain it. And all those – oblique questions you asked me –

**Hedda**    You knew what they meant.

56   Hedda Gabler

**Loevborg**   But that you could sit there and ask me such questions! So unashamedly –

**Hedda**   I thought you said they were oblique.

**Loevborg**   Yes, but you asked them so unashamedly. That you could question me about – about that kind of thing!

**Hedda**   You answered willingly enough.

**Loevborg**   Yes – that's what I can't understand – looking back on it. But tell me, Hedda – what you felt for me – wasn't that – love? When you asked me those questions and made me confess my sins to you, wasn't it because you wanted to wash me clean?

**Hedda**   No, not exactly.

**Loevborg**   Why did you do it, then?

**Hedda**   Do you find it so incredible that a young girl, given the chance in secret, should want to be allowed a glimpse into a forbidden world of whose existence she is supposed to be ignorant?

**Loevborg**   So that was it?

**Hedda**   One reason. One reason – I think.

**Loevborg**   You didn't love me, then. You just wanted – knowledge. But if that was so, why did you break it off?

**Hedda**   That was your fault.

**Loevborg**   It was you who put an end to it.

**Hedda**   Yes, when I realized that our friendship was threatening to develop into something – something else. Shame on you, Eilert Loevborg! How could you abuse the trust of your dearest friend?

**Loevborg** (*clenches his fist*)   Oh, why didn't you do it? Why didn't you shoot me dead? As you threatened to!

**Hedda**   I was afraid. Of the scandal.

**Loevborg**   Yes, Hedda. You're a coward at heart.

**Hedda**   A dreadful coward. (*Changes her tone.*) Luckily for you. Well, now you've found consolation with the Elvsteds.

**Loevborg**   I know what Thea's been telling you.

**Hedda**   I dare say you told her about us.

**Loevborg**   Not a word. She's too silly to understand that kind of thing.

**Hedda**   Silly?

**Loevborg**   She's silly about that kind of thing.

**Hedda**   And I'm a coward. (*Leans closer to him, without looking him in the eyes, and says quietly.*) But let me tell you something. Something you don't know.

**Loevborg** (*tensely*)   Yes?

**Hedda**   My failure to shoot you wasn't my worst act of cowardice that evening.

**Loevborg** (*looks at her for a moment, realizes her meaning, and whispers passionately*)   Oh, Hedda! Hedda Gabler! Now I see what was behind those questions. Yes! It wasn't knowledge you wanted! It was life! learn what man is about, and how... [handwritten annotation]

**Hedda** (*flashes a look at him and says quietly*)   Take care! Don't you delude yourself!

*It has begun to grow dark.* **Bertha**, *from outside, opens the door leading into the hall.*

**Hedda** (*closes the album with a snap and cries, smiling*)   Ah, at last! Come in, Thea dear!

**Mrs Elvsted** *enters from the hall, in evening dress. The door is closed behind her.*

**Hedda** (*on the sofa, stretches out her arms towards her*)   Thea darling, I thought you were never coming!

**Mrs Elvsted** *makes a slight bow to the gentlemen in the rear room as she passes the open doorway, and then to her. Then she goes to the*

*table and holds out her hand to* **Hedda**. **Eilert Loevborg** *has risen from his chair. He and* **Mrs Elvsted** *nod silently to each other.*

**Mrs Elvsted**   Perhaps I ought to go in and say a few words to your husband?

**Hedda**   Oh, there's no need. They're happy by themselves. They'll be going soon.

**Mrs Elvsted**   Going?

**Hedda**   Yes, they're off on a spree this evening.

**Mrs Elvsted** (*quickly, to* **Loevborg**)   You're not going with them?

**Loevborg**   No.

**Hedda**   Mr Loevborg is staying here with us.

**Mrs Elvsted** (*takes a chair and is about to sit down beside him*) Oh, how nice it is to be here!

**Hedda**   No, Thea darling, not there. Come over here and sit beside me. I want to be in the middle.

**Mrs Elvsted**   Yes, just as you wish.

*She goes round the table and sits on the sofa, on* **Hedda**'s *right.* **Loevborg** *sits down again in his chair.*

**Loevborg** (*after a short pause, to* **Hedda**)   Isn't she lovely to look at?

**Hedda** (*strokes her hair gently*)   Only to look at?

**Loevborg**   Yes. We're just good friends. We trust each other implicitly. We can talk to each other quite unashamedly.

**Hedda**   No need to be oblique?

**Mrs Elvsted** (*nestles close to* **Hedda** *and says quietly*)   Oh, Hedda, I'm so happy. Imagine – he says I've inspired him!

**Hedda** (*looks at her with a smile*)   Dear Thea! Does he really?

**Loevborg**   She has the courage of her convictions, Mrs Tesman.

**Mrs Elvsted**   I? Courage?

**Loevborg**   Absolute courage. Where friendship is concerned.

**Hedda**   Yes. Courage. Yes. If only one had that –

**Loevborg**   Yes?

**Hedda**   One might be able to live. In spite of everything. (*Changes her tone suddenly.*) Well, Thea darling, now you're going to drink a nice glass of cold punch.

**Mrs Elvsted**   No thank you. I never drink anything like that.

**Hedda**   Oh. You, Mr Loevborg?

**Loevborg**   Thank you, I don't either.

**Mrs Elvsted**   No, he doesn't, either.

**Hedda** (*looks into his eyes*)   But if I want you to.

**Loevborg**   That doesn't make any difference.

**Hedda** (*laughs*)   Have I no power over you at all? Poor me!

**Loevborg**   Not where this is concerned.

**Hedda**   Seriously, I think you should. For your own sake.

**Mrs Elvsted**   Hedda!

**Loevborg**   Why?

**Hedda**   Or perhaps I should say for other people's sake.

**Loevborg**   What do you mean?

**Hedda**   People might think you didn't feel absolutely and unashamedly sure of yourself. In your heart of hearts.

**Mrs Elvsted** (*quietly*)   Oh, Hedda, no!

**Loevborg**   People can think what they like. For the

present.

**Mrs Elvsted** (*happily*)   Yes, that's true.

**Hedda**   I saw it so clearly in Judge Brack a few minutes ago.

**Loevborg**   Oh. What did you see?

**Hedda**   He smiled so scornfully when he saw you were afraid to go in there and drink with them.

**Loevborg**   Afraid! I wanted to stay here and talk to you.

**Mrs Elvsted**   That was only natural, Hedda.

**Hedda**   But the Judge wasn't to know that. I saw him wink at Tesman when you showed you didn't dare to join their wretched little party.

**Loevborg**   Didn't dare! Are you saying I didn't dare?

**Hedda**   I'm not saying so. But that was what Judge Brack thought.

**Loevborg**   Well, let him.

**Hedda**   You're not going, then?

**Loevborg**   I'm staying here with you and Thea.

**Mrs Elvsted**   Yes, Hedda, of course he is.

**Hedda** (*smiles, and nods approvingly to* **Loevborg**)   Firm as a rock! A man of principle! That's how a man should be! (*Turns to* **Mrs Elvsted** *and strokes her cheek.*) Didn't I tell you so this morning when you came here in such a panic – ?

**Loevborg** (*starts*)   Panic?

**Mrs Elvsted** (*frightened*)   Hedda! But – Hedda!

**Hedda**   Well, now you can see for yourself. There's no earthly need for you to get scared to death just because – (*Stops.*) Well! Let's all three cheer up and enjoy ourselves.

**Loevborg**   Mrs Tesman, would you mind explaining to me what this is all about?

**Mrs Elvsted** Oh, my God, my God, Hedda, what are you saying? What are you doing?

**Hedda** Keep calm. That horrid Judge has his eye on you.

**Loevborg** Scared to death, were you? For my sake?

**Mrs Elvsted** (*quietly, trembling*) Oh, Hedda! You've made me so unhappy!

**Loevborg** (*looks coldly at her for a moment. His face is distorted*) So that was how much you trusted me.

**Mrs Elvsted** Eilert dear, please listen to me –

**Loevborg** (*takes one of the glasses of punch, raises it and says quietly, hoarsely*) Skoal, Thea!

*He empties the glass, puts it down and picks up one of the others.*

**Mrs Elvsted** (*quietly*) Hedda, Hedda! Why did you want this to happen?

**Hedda** *I* – want it? Are you mad?

**Loevborg** Skoal to you, too, Mrs Tesman. Thanks for telling me the truth. Here's to the truth!

*He empties his glass and refills it.*

**Hedda** (*puts her hand on his arm*) Steady. That's enough for now. Don't forget the party.

**Mrs Elvsted** No, no, no!

**Hedda** Ssh! They're looking at you.

**Loevborg** (*puts down his glass*) Thea, tell me the truth –

**Mrs Elvsted** Yes!

**Loevborg** Did your husband know you were following me?

**Mrs Elvsted** Oh, Hedda!

**Loevborg** Did you and he have an agreement that you should come here and keep an eye on me? Perhaps he

gave you the idea? After all, he's a magistrate. I suppose he needed me back in his office. Or did he miss my companionship at the card-table?

**Mrs Elvsted** (*quietly, sobbing*)   Eilert, Eilert!

**Loevborg** (*seizes a glass and is about to fill it*)   Let's drink to him, too.

**Hedda**   No more now. Remember you're going to read your book to Tesman.

**Loevborg** (*calm again, puts down his glass*)   That was silly of me, Thea. To take it like that, I mean. Don't be angry with me, my dear. You'll see – yes, and they'll see, too – that though I fell, I – I have raised myself up again. With your help, Thea.

**Mrs Elvsted** (*happily*)   Oh, thank God!

**Brack** *has meanwhile glanced at his watch. He and* **Tesman** *get up and come into the drawing-room.*

**Brack** (*takes his hat and overcoat*)   Well, Mrs Tesman, it's time for us to go.

**Hedda**   Yes, I suppose it must be.

**Loevborg** (*gets up*)   Time for me, too, Judge.

**Mrs Elvsted** (*quietly, pleadingly*)   Eilert, please don't!

**Hedda** (*pinches her arm*)   They can hear you.

**Mrs Elvsted** (*gives a little cry*)   Oh!

**Loevborg** (*to* **Brack**)   You were kind enough to ask me to join you.

**Brack**   Are you coming?

**Loevborg**   If I may.

**Brack**   Delighted.

**Loevborg** (*puts the paper package in his pocket and says to* **Tesman**)   I'd like to show you one or two things before I send it off to the printer.

**Tesman**   I say, that'll be fun. Fancy – ! Oh, but, Hedda, how'll Mrs Elvsted get home? What?

**Hedda**   Oh, we'll manage somehow.

**Loevborg** (*glances over towards the ladies*)   Mrs Elvsted? I shall come back and collect her, naturally. (*Goes closer.*) About ten o'clock, Mrs Tesman? Will that suit you?

**Hedda**   Yes. That'll suit me admirably.

**Tesman**   Good, that's settled. But you mustn't expect me back so early, Hedda.

**Hedda**   Stay as long as you c – as long as you like, dear.

**Mrs Elvsted** (*trying to hide her anxiety*)   Well then, Mr Loevborg, I'll wait here till you come.

**Loevborg** (*his hat in his hand*)   Pray do, Mrs Elvsted.

**Brack**   Well, gentlemen, now the party begins. I trust that, in the words of a certain fair lady, we shall enjoy good sport.

**Hedda**   What a pity the fair lady can't be there, invisible.

**Brack**   Why invisible?

**Hedda**   So as to be able to hear some of your uncensored witticisms, your honour.

**Brack** (*laughs*)   Oh, I shouldn't advise the fair lady to do that.

**Tesman** (*laughs, too*)   I say, Hedda, that's good. What!

**Brack**   Well, good night, ladies, good night!

**Loevborg** (*bows farewell*)   About ten o'clock then.

**Brack**, **Loevborg** and **Tesman** *go out through the hall. As they do so,* **Bertha** *enters from the rear room with a lighted lamp. She puts it on the drawing-room table, then goes out the way she came.*

**Mrs Elvsted** (*has got up and is walking uneasily to and fro*)   Oh, Hedda, Hedda! How is all this going to end?

**Hedda** At ten o'clock, then. He'll be here. I can see him. With a crown of vine leaves in his hair. Burning and unashamed!

**Mrs Elvsted** Oh, I do hope so!

**Hedda** Can't you see? Then he'll be himself again! He'll be a free man for the rest of his days!

**Mrs Elvsted** Please God you're right.

**Hedda** That's how he'll come! (*Gets up and goes closer.*) You can doubt him as much as you like. I believe in him! Now we'll see which of us –

**Mrs Elvsted** You're after something, Hedda.

**Hedda** Yes, I am. For once in my life I want to have the power to shape a man's destiny.

**Mrs Elvsted** Haven't you that power already?

**Hedda** No, I haven't. I've never had it.

**Mrs Elvsted** What about your husband?

**Hedda** Him! Oh, if you could only understand how poor I am. And you're allowed to be so rich, so rich! (*Clasps her passionately.*) I think I'll burn your hair off after all!

**Mrs Elvsted** Let me go! Let me go! You frighten me, Hedda!

**Bertha** (*in the open doorway*) I've laid tea in the dining-room, madam.

**Hedda** Good, we're coming.

**Mrs Elvsted** No, no, no! I'd rather go home alone! Now – at once!

**Hedda** Rubbish! First you're going to have some tea, you little idiot. And then – at ten o'clock – Eilert Loevborg will come. With a crown of vine leaves in his hair!

*She drags* **Mrs Elvsted** *almost forcibly towards the open doorway.*

# Act Three

*The same. The curtains are drawn across the open doorway, and also across the french windows. The lamp, half turned down, with a shade over it, is burning on the table. In the stove, the door of which is open, a fire has been burning, but it is now almost out.* **Mrs Elvsted**, *wrapped in a large shawl and with her feet resting on a footstool, is sitting near the stove, huddled in the armchair.* **Hedda** *is lying asleep on the sofa, fully dressed, with a blanket over her.*

**Mrs Elvsted** (*after a pause, suddenly sits up in her chair and listens tensely. Then she sinks wearily back again and sighs*)  Not back yet! Oh, God! Oh, God! Not back yet!

**Bertha** *tiptoes cautiously in from the hall. She has a letter in her hand.*

**Mrs Elvsted** (*turns and whispers*)  What is it? Has someone come?

**Bertha** (*quietly*)  Yes, a servant's just called with this letter.

**Mrs Elvsted** (*quickly, holding out her hand*)  A letter! Give it to me!

**Bertha**  But it's for the Doctor, madam.

**Mrs Elvsted**  Oh, I see.

**Bertha**  Miss Tesman's maid brought it. I'll leave it here on the table.

**Mrs Elvsted**  Yes, do.

**Bertha** (*puts down the letter*)  I'd better put the lamp out. It's starting to smoke.

**Mrs Elvsted**  Yes, put it out. It'll soon be daylight.

**Bertha** (*puts out the lamp*)  It's daylight already, madam.

**Mrs Elvsted**  Yes. Broad day. And not home yet.

**Bertha**  Oh dear, I was afraid this would happen.

**Mrs Elvsted**   Were you?

**Bertha**   Yes. When I heard that a certain gentleman had returned to town, and saw him go off with them. I've heard all about him.

**Mrs Elvsted**   Don't talk so loud. You'll wake your mistress.

**Bertha** (*looks at the sofa and sighs*)   Yes. Let her go on sleeping, poor dear. Shall I put some more wood on the fire?

**Mrs Elvsted**   Thank you, don't bother on my account.

**Bertha**   Very good.

*She goes quietly out through the hall.*

**Hedda** (*wakes as the door closes and looks up*)   What's that?

**Mrs Elvsted**   It was only the maid.

**Hedda** (*looks round*)   What am I doing here? Oh, now I remember. (*Sits up on the sofa, stretches herself and rubs her eyes.*) What time is it, Thea?

**Mrs Elvsted**   It's gone seven.

**Hedda**   When did Tesman get back?

**Mrs Elvsted**   He's not back yet.

**Hedda**   Not home yet?

**Mrs Elvsted** (*gets up*)   No one's come.

**Hedda**   And we sat up waiting for them till four o'clock.

**Mrs Elvsted**   God! How I waited for him!

**Hedda** (*yawns and says with her hand in front of her mouth*) Oh, dear. We might have saved ourselves the trouble.

**Mrs Elvsted**   Did you manage to sleep?

**Hedda**   Oh, yes. Quite well, I think. Didn't you get any?

**Mrs Elvsted**   Not a wink. I couldn't, Hedda. I just

couldn't.

**Hedda** (*gets up and comes over to her*) Now, now, now. There's nothing to worry about. I know what's happened.

**Mrs Elvsted** What? Please tell me.

**Hedda** Well, obviously the party went on very late –

**Mrs Elvsted** Oh dear, I suppose it must have. But –

**Hedda** And Tesman didn't want to come home and wake us all up in the middle of the night. (*Laughs.*) Probably wasn't too keen to show his face either, after a spree like that.

**Mrs Elvsted** But where could he have gone?

**Hedda** I should think he's probably slept at his aunts'. They keep his old room for him.

**Mrs Elvsted** No, he can't be with them. A letter came for him just now from Miss Tesman. It's over there.

**Hedda** Oh? (*Looks at the envelope.*) Yes, it's Auntie Juju's handwriting. Well, he must still be at Judge Brack's, then. And Eilert Loevborg is sitting there, reading to him. With a crown of vine leaves in his hair.

**Mrs Elvsted** Hedda, you're only saying that. You don't believe it.

**Hedda** Thea, you really are a little fool.

**Mrs Elvsted** Perhaps I am.

**Hedda** You look tired to death.

**Mrs Elvsted** Yes. I am tired to death.

**Hedda** Go to my room and lie down for a little. Do as I say, now; don't argue.

**Mrs Elvsted** No, no. I couldn't possibly sleep.

**Hedda** Of course you can.

**Mrs Elvsted** But your husband'll be home soon. And I

must know at once –

**Hedda**   I'll tell you when he comes.

**Mrs Elvsted**   Promise me, Hedda?

**Hedda**   Yes, don't worry. Go and get some sleep.

**Mrs Elvsted**   Thank you. All right, I'll try.

*She goes out through the rear room.* **Hedda** *goes to the french windows and draws the curtains. Broad daylight floods into the room. She goes to the writing-table, takes a small hand-mirror from it and arranges her hair. Then she goes to the door leading into the hall and presses the bell. After a few moments,* **Bertha** *enters.*

**Bertha**   Did you want anything, madam?

**Hedda**   Yes, put some more wood on the fire. I'm freezing.

**Bertha**   Bless you, I'll soon have this room warmed up. (*She rakes the embers together and puts a fresh piece of wood on them. Suddenly she stops and listens.*) There's someone at the front door, madam.

**Hedda**   Well, go and open it. I'll see to the fire.

**Bertha**   It'll burn up in moment.

*She goes out through the hall.* **Hedda** *kneels on the footstool and puts more wood in the stove. After a few seconds,* **George Tesman** *enters from the hall. He looks tired, and rather worried. He tiptoes towards the open doorway and is about to slip through the curtains.*

**Hedda** (*at the stove, without looking up*)   Good morning.

**Tesman** (*turns*)   Hedda! (*Comes nearer.*) Good heavens, are you up already? What?

**Hedda**   Yes. I got up very early this morning.

**Tesman**   I was sure you'd still be sleeping. Fancy that!

**Hedda**   Don't talk so loud. Mrs Elvsted's asleep in my room.

**Tesman**   Mrs Elvsted? Has she stayed the night here?

**Hedda**   Yes. No one came to escort her home.

**Tesman**   Oh. No, I suppose not.

**Hedda** (*closes the door of the stove and gets up*)   Well. Was it fun?

**Tesman**   Have you been anxious about me? What?

**Hedda**   Not in the least. I asked if you'd had fun.

**Tesman**   Oh yes, rather! Well, I thought, for once in a while – ! The first part was the best; when Eilert read his book to me. We arrived over an hour too early – what about that, eh? Fancy – ! Brack had a lot of things to see to, so Eilert read to me.

**Hedda** (*sits at the right-hand side of the table*)   Well? Tell me about it.

**Tesman** (*sits on a footstool by the stove*)   Honestly, Hedda, you've no idea what a book that's going to be. It's really one of the most remarkable things that's ever been written. By Jove!

**Hedda**   Oh, never mind about the book –

**Tesman**   I'm going to make a confession to you, Hedda. When he'd finished reading a sort of beastly feeling came over me.

**Hedda**   Beastly feeling?

**Tesman**   I found myself envying Eilert for being able to write like that. Imagine that, Hedda!

**Hedda**   Yes. I can imagine.

**Tesman**   What a tragedy that with all those gifts he should be so incorrigible.

**Hedda**   You mean he's less afraid of life than most men?

**Tesman**   Good heavens, no. He just doesn't know the meaning of the word moderation.

**Hedda**   What happened afterwards?

**Tesman**   Well, looking back on it, I suppose you might almost call it an orgy, Hedda.

**Hedda**   Had he vine leaves in his hair?

**Tesman**   Vine leaves? No, I didn't see any of them. He made a long, rambling oration in honour of the woman who'd inspired him to write this book. Yes, those were the words he used.

**Hedda**   Did he name her?

**Tesman**   No. But I suppose it must be Mrs Elvsted. You wait and see!

**Hedda**   Where did you leave him?

**Tesman**   On the way home. We left in a bunch – the last of us, that is – and Brack came with us to get a little fresh air. Well, then, you see, we agreed we ought to see Eilert home. He'd had a drop too much.

**Hedda**   You don't say?

**Tesman**   But now comes the funny part, Hedda. Or I should really say the tragic part. Oh, I'm almost ashamed to tell you. For Eilert's sake, I mean –

**Hedda**   Why, what happened?

**Tesman**   Well, you see, as we were walking towards town I happened to drop behind for a minute. Only for a minute – er – you understand –

**Hedda**   Yes, yes – ?

**Tesman**   Well then, when I ran on to catch them up, what do you think I found by the roadside. What?

**Hedda**   How on earth should I know?

**Tesman**   You mustn't tell anyone, Hedda. What? Promise me that – for Eilert's sake. (*Takes a package wrapped in paper from his coat pocket.*) Just fancy! I found this.

**Hedda**   Isn't this the one he brought here yesterday?

**Tesman**   Yes! The whole of that precious, irreplaceable manuscript! And he went and lost it! Didn't even notice! What about that? Tragic.

**Hedda**   But why didn't you give it back to him?

**Tesman**   I didn't dare to, in the state he was in.

**Hedda**   Didn't you tell any of the others?

**Tesman**   Good heavens, no. I didn't want to do that. For Eilert's sake, you understand.

**Hedda**   Then no one else knows you have his manuscript?

**Tesman**   No. And no one must be allowed to know.

**Hedda**   Didn't it come up in the conversation later?

**Tesman**   I didn't get a chance to talk to him any more. As soon as we got into the outskirts of town, he and one or two of the others gave us the slip. Disappeared, by Jove!

**Hedda**   Oh? I suppose they took him home.

**Tesman**   Yes, I imagine that was the idea. Brack left us, too.

**Hedda**   And what have you been up to since then?

**Tesman**   Well, I and one or two of the others – awfully jolly chaps, they were – went back to where one of them lived and had a cup of morning coffee. Morning-after coffee – what? Ah, well. I'll just lie down for a bit and give Eilert time to sleep it off, poor chap, then I'll run over and give this back to him.

**Hedda** (*holds out her hand for the package*   No, don't do that. Not just yet. Let me read it first.

**Tesman**   Oh no, really, Hedda dear, honestly, I daren't do that.

**Hedda**   Daren't?

**Tesman**   No – imagine how desperate he'll be when he wakes up and finds his manuscript's missing. He hasn't any copy, you see. He told me so himself.

**Hedda**   Can't a thing like that be rewritten?

**Tesman**   Oh no, not possibly, I shouldn't think. I mean, the inspiration, you know –

**Hedda**   Oh, yes, I'd forgotten that. (*Casually.*) By the way, there's a letter for you.

**Tesman**   Is there? Fancy that!

**Hedda** (*holds it out to him*)   It came early this morning.

**Tesman**   I say, it's from Auntie Juju! What on earth can it be? (*Puts the package on the other footstool, opens the letter, reads it and jumps up.*) Oh, Hedda! She says poor Auntie Rena's dying.

**Hedda**   Well, we've been expecting that.

**Tesman**   She says if I want to see her I must go quickly. I'll run over at once.

**Hedda** (*hides a smile*)   Run?

**Tesman**   Hedda dear, I suppose you wouldn't like to come with me? What about that, eh?

**Hedda** (*gets up and says wearily and with repulsion*)   No, no, don't ask me to do anything like that. I can't bear illness or death. I loathe anything ugly.

**Tesman**   Yes, yes. Of course. (*In a dither.*) My hat? My overcoat? Oh yes, in the hall. I do hope I won't get there too late, Hedda! What?

**Hedda**   You'll be all right if you run.

**Bertha** *enters from the hall.*

**Bertha**   Judge Brack's outside and wants to know if he can come in.

**Tesman**   At this hour? No, I can't possibly receive him

now.

**Hedda**   I can. (*To* **Bertha**.) Ask his honour to come in.

**Bertha** *goes.*

**Hedda** (*whispers quickly*)   The manuscript, Tesman.

*She snatches it from the footstool.*

**Tesman**   Yes, give it to me.

**Hedda**   No, I'll look after it for now.

*She goes over to the writing-table and puts it in the bookcase.*
**Tesman** *stands dithering, unable to get his gloves on.* **Judge Brack** *enters from the hall.*

(*Nods to him.*) Well, you're an early bird.

**Brack**   Yes, aren't I? (*To* **Tesman**.) Are you up and about, too?

**Tesman**   Yes, I've got to go and see my aunts. Poor Auntie Rena's dying.

**Brack**   Oh dear, is she? Then you mustn't let me detain you. At so tragic a –

**Tesman**   Yes, I really must run. Goodbye! Goodbye!

*He runs out through the hall.*

**Hedda** (*goes nearer*)   You seem to have had excellent sport last night – Judge.

**Brack**   Indeed yes, Mrs Hedda. I haven't even had time to take my clothes off.

**Hedda**   *You* haven't either?

**Brack**   As you see. What's Tesman told you about last night's escapades?

**Hedda**   Oh, only some boring story about having gone and drunk coffee somewhere.

**Brack**   Yes, I've heard about that coffee-party. Eilert Loevborg wasn't with them, I gather?

**Hedda**   No, they took him home first.

**Brack**   Did Tesman go with him?

**Hedda**   No, one or two of the others, he said.

**Brack** (*smiles*)   George Tesman is a credulous man, Mrs Hedda.

**Hedda**   God knows. But – has something happened?

**Brack**   Well, yes, I'm afraid it has.

**Hedda**   I see. Sit down and tell me.

*She sits on the left of the table,* **Brack** *at the long side of it, near her.*

Well?

**Brack**   I had a special reason for keeping track of my guests last night. Or perhaps I should say some of my guests.

**Hedda**   Including Eilert Loevborg?

**Brack**   I must confess – yes.

**Hedda**   You're beginning to make me curious.

**Brack**   Do you know where he and some of my other guests spent the latter half of last night, Mrs Hedda?

**Hedda**   Tell me. If it won't shock me.

**Brack**   Oh, I don't think it'll shock you. They found themselves participating in an exceedingly animated *soirée*.

**Hedda**   Of a sporting character?

**Brack**   Of a highly sporting character.

**Hedda**   Tell me more.

**Brack**   Loevborg had received an invitation in advance – as had the others. I knew all about that. But he had refused. As you know, he's become a new man.

**Hedda**   Up at the Elvsteds', yes. But he went?

**Brack**  Well, you see, Mrs Hedda, last night at my house, unhappily, the spirit moved him.

**Hedda**  Yes, I hear he became inspired.

**Brack**  Somewhat violently inspired. And as a result, I suppose, his thoughts strayed. We men, alas, don't always stick to our principles as firmly as we should.

**Hedda**  I'm sure you're an exception, Judge Brack. But go on about Loevborg.

**Brack**  Well, to cut a long story short, he ended up in the establishment of a certain Mademoiselle Danielle.

**Hedda**  Mademoiselle Danielle?

**Brack**  She was holding the *soirée*. For a selected circle of friends and admirers.

**Hedda**  Has she got red hair?

**Brack**  She has.

**Hedda**  A singer of some kind?

**Brack**  Yes – among other accomplishments. She's also a celebrated huntress – of men, Mrs Hedda. I'm sure you've heard about her. Eilert Loevborg used to be one of her most ardent patrons. In his salad days.

**Hedda**  And how did all this end?

**Brack**  Not entirely amicably, from all accounts. Mademoiselle Danielle began by receiving him with the utmost tenderness and ended by resorting to her fists.

**Hedda**  Against Loevborg?

**Brack**  Yes. He accused her, or her friends, of having robbed him. He claimed his pocket-book had been stolen. Among other things. In short, he seems to have made a blood-thirsty scene.

**Hedda**  And what did this lead to?

**Brack**  It led to a general free-for-all, in which both sexes

participated. Fortunately, in the end the police arrived.

**Hedda**   The police, too?

**Brack**   Yes. I'm afraid it may turn out to be rather an expensive joke for Master Eilert. Crazy fool!

**Hedda**   Oh?

**Brack**   Apparently he put up a very violent resistance. Hit one of the constables on the ear and tore his uniform. He had to accompany them to the police station.

**Hedda**   Where did you learn all this?

**Brack**   From the police.

**Hedda** (*to herself*)   So that's what happened. He didn't have a crown of vine leaves in his hair.

**Brack**   Vine leaves, Mrs Hedda?

**Hedda** (*in her normal voice again*)   But, tell me, Judge, why do you take such a close interest in Eilert Loevborg?

**Brack**   For one thing it'll hardly be a matter of complete indifference to me if it's revealed in court that he came there straight from my house.

**Hedda**   Will it come to court?

**Brack**   Of course. Well, I don't regard that as particularly serious. Still, I thought it my duty, as a friend of the family, to give you and your husband a full account of his nocturnal adventures.

**Hedda**   Why?

**Brack**   Because I've a shrewd suspicion that he's hoping to use you as a kind of screen.

**Hedda**   What makes you think that?

**Brack**   Oh, for heaven's sake, Mrs Hedda, we're not blind. You wait and see. This Mrs Elvsted won't be going back to her husband just yet.

**Hedda**   Well, if there were anything between those two

there are plenty of other places where they could meet.

**Brack**   Not in anyone's home. From now on every respectable house will once again be closed to Eilert Loevborg.

**Hedda**   And mine should be, too, you mean?

**Brack**   Yes. I confess I should find it more than irksome if this gentleman were to be granted unrestricted access to this house. If he were superfluously to intrude into –

**Hedda**   The triangle?

**Brack**   Precisely. For me it would be like losing a home.

**Hedda** (*looks at him and smiles*)   I see. You want to be the cock of the walk.

**Brack** (*nods slowly and lowers his voice*)   Yes, that is my aim. And I shall fight for it with – every weapon at my disposal.

**Hedda** (*as her smile fades*)   You're a dangerous man, aren't you? When you really want something.

**Brack**   You think so?

**Hedda**   Yes, I'm beginning to think so. I'm deeply thankful you haven't any kind of hold over me.

**Brack** (*laughs equivocally*)   Well, well, Mrs Hedda – perhaps you're right. If I had, who knows what I might not think up?

**Hedda**   Come, Judge Brack. That sounds almost like a threat.

**Brack** (*gets up*)   Heaven forbid! In the creation of a triangle – and its continuance – the question of compulsion should never arise.

**Hedda**   Exactly what I was thinking.

**Brack**   Well, I've said what I came to say. I must be getting back. Goodbye, Mrs Hedda. (*Goes towards the french windows.*)

**Hedda** (*gets up*)   Are you going out through the garden?

**Brack**   Yes, it's shorter.

**Hedda**   Yes. And it's the back door, isn't it?

**Brack**   I've nothing against back doors. They can be quite intriguing – sometimes.

**Hedda**   When people fire pistols out of them, for example?

**Brack** (*in the doorway, laughs*)   Oh, people don't shoot tame cocks.

**Hedda** (*laughs, too*)   I suppose not. When they've only got one.

*They nod goodbye, laughing. He goes. She closes the french windows behind him, and stands for a moment, looking out pensively. Then she walks across the room and glances through the curtains in the open doorway. Goes to the writing-table, takes* **Loevborg**'s *package from the bookcase and is about to turn through the pages when* **Bertha** *is heard remonstrating loudly in the hall.* **Hedda** *turns and listens. She hastily puts the package back in the drawer, locks it and puts the key on the inkstand.* **Eilert Loevborg**, *with his overcoat on and his hat in his hand, throws the door open. He looks somewhat confused and excited.*

**Loevborg** (*shouts as he enters*)   I must come in, I tell you! Let me pass!

*He closes the door, turns, sees* **Hedda**, *controls himself immediately and bows.*

**Hedda** (*at the writing-table*)   Well, Mr Loevborg, this is rather a late hour to be collecting Thea.

**Loevborg**   And an early hour to call on you. Please forgive me.

**Hedda**   How do you know she's still here?

**Loevborg**   They told me at her lodgings that she has been out all night.

**Hedda** (*goes to the table*)  Did you notice anything about their behaviour when they told you?

**Loevborg** (*looks at her, puzzled*)  Notice anything?

**Hedda**  Did they sound as if they thought it – strange?

**Loevborg** (*suddenly understands*)  Oh, I see what you mean. I'm dragging her down with me. No, as a matter of fact I didn't notice anything. I suppose Tesman isn't up yet?

**Hedda**  No, I don't think so.

**Loevborg**  When did he get home?

**Hedda**  Very late.

**Loevborg**  Did he tell you anything?

**Hedda**  Yes. I gather you had a merry party at Judge Brack's last night.

**Loevborg**  He didn't tell you anything else?

**Hedda**  I don't think so. I was so terribly sleepy –

**Mrs Elvsted** *comes through the curtains in the open doorway.*

**Mrs Elvsted** (*runs towards him*)  Oh, Eilert! At last!

**Loevborg**  Yes – at last. And too late.

**Mrs Elvsted**  What is too late?

**Loevborg**  Everything – now. I'm finished, Thea.

**Mrs Elvsted**  Oh, no, no! Don't say that!

**Loevborg**  You'll say it yourself, when you've heard what I –

**Mrs Elvsted**  I don't want to hear anything!

**Hedda**  Perhaps you'd rather speak to her alone? I'd better go.

**Loevborg**  No, stay.

**Mrs Elvsted**  But I don't want to hear anything, I tell you!

**Loevborg**   It's not about last night.

**Mrs Elvsted**   Then what – ?

**Loevborg**   I want to tell you that from now on we must stop seeing each other.

**Mrs Elvsted**   Stop seeing each other!

**Hedda** (*involuntarily*)   I knew it!

**Loevborg**   I have no further use for you, Thea.

**Mrs Elvsted**   You can stand there and say that! No further use for me! Surely I can go on helping you? We'll go on working together, won't we?

**Loevborg**   I don't intend to do any more work from now on.

**Mrs Elvsted** (*desperately*)   Then what use have I for my life?

**Loevborg**   You must try to live as if you had never known me.

**Mrs Elvsted**   But I can't!

**Loevborg**   Try to, Thea. Go back home –

**Mrs Elvsted**   Never! I want to be wherever you are! I won't let myself be driven away like this! I want to stay here – and be with you when the book comes out.

**Hedda** (*whispers*)   Ah, yes! The book!

**Loevborg** (*looks at her*)   Our book; Thea's and mine. It belongs to both of us.

**Mrs Elvsted**   Oh, yes! I feel that, too! And I've a right to be with you when it comes into the world. I want to see people respect and honour you again. And the joy! The joy! I want to share it with you!

**Loevborg**   Thea – our book will never come into the world.

**Hedda**   Ah!

**Mrs Elvsted**  Not – ?

**Loevborg**  It cannot. Ever.

**Mrs Elvsted**  Eilert – what have you done with the manuscript?

**Hedda**  Yes – the manuscript?

**Mrs Elvsted**  Where is it?

**Loevborg**  Oh, Thea, please don't ask me that!

**Mrs Elvsted**  Yes, yes – I must know. I've a right to know. Now!

**Loevborg**  The manuscript. Yes. I've torn it up.

**Mrs Elvsted**  (*screams*)  No, no!

**Hedda**  (*involuntarily*)  But that's not – !

**Loevborg**  (*looks at her*)  Not true, you think.

**Hedda**  (*controls herself*)  Why – yes, of course it is, if you say so. It sounded so incredible –

**Loevborg**  It's true, nevertheless.

**Mrs Elvsted**  Oh, my God, my God, Hedda – he's destroyed his own book!

**Loevborg**  I have destroyed my life. Why not my life's work, too?

**Mrs Elvsted**  And you – did this last night?

**Loevborg**  Yes, Thea. I tore it into a thousand pieces. And scattered them out across the fjord. It's good, clean, salt water. Let it carry them away; let them drift in the current and the wind. And in a little while, they will sink. Deeper and deeper. As I shall, Thea.

**Mrs Elvsted**  Do you know, Eilert – this book – all my life I shall feel as though you'd killed a little child?

**Loevborg**  You're right. It is like killing a child.

**Mrs Elvsted**  But how could you? It was my child, too!

**Hedda** (*almost inaudibly*)   Oh – the child – !

**Mrs Elvsted** (*breathes heavily*)   It's all over, then. Well – I'll go now, Hedda.

**Hedda**   You're not leaving town?

**Mrs Elvsted**   I don't know what I'm going to do. I can't see anything except – darkness.

*She goes out through the hall.*

**Hedda** (*waits a moment*)   Aren't you going to escort her home, Mr Loevborg?

**Loevborg**   I? Through the streets? Do you want me to let people see her with me?

**Hedda**   Of course, I don't know what else may have happened last night. But is it so utterly beyond redress?

**Loevborg**   It isn't just last night. It'll go on happening. I know it. But the curse of it is, I don't want to live that kind of life. I don't want to start all that again. She's broken my courage. I can't spit in the eyes of the world any longer.

**Hedda** (*as though to herself*)   That pretty little fool's been trying to shape a man's destiny. (*Looks at him.*) But how could you be so heartless towards her?

**Loevborg**   Don't call me heartless!

**Hedda**   To go and destroy the one thing that's made her life worth living? You don't call that heartless?

**Loevborg**   Do you want to know the truth, Hedda?

**Hedda**   The truth?

**Loevborg**   Promise me first – give me your word – that you'll never let Thea know about this.

**Hedda**   I give you my word.

**Loevborg**   Good. Well; what I told her just now was a lie.

**Hedda**  About the manuscript?

**Loevborg**  Yes. I didn't tear it up. Or throw it in the fjord.

**Hedda**  You didn't? But where is it, then?

**Loevborg**  I destroyed it, all the same. I destroyed it, Hedda!

**Hedda**  I don't understand.

**Loevborg**  Thea said that what I had done was like killing a child.

**Hedda**  Yes. That's what she said.

**Loevborg**  But to kill a child isn't the worst thing a father can do to it.

**Hedda**  What could be worse than that?

**Loevborg**  Hedda – suppose a man came home one morning, after a night of debauchery, and said to the mother of his child: 'Look here. I've been wandering round all night. I've been to – such-and-such a place and such-and-such a place. And I had our child with me. I took him to – these places. And I've lost him. Just – lost him. God knows where he is or whose hands he's fallen into.'

**Hedda**  I see. But when all's said and done, this was only a book –

**Loevborg**  Thea's heart and soul were in that book. It was her whole life.

**Hedda**  Yes, I understand.

**Loevborg**  Well, then you must also understand that she and I cannot possibly ever see each other again.

**Hedda**  Where will you go?

**Loevborg**  Nowhere. I just want to put an end to it all. As soon as possible.

**Hedda** (*takes a step towards him*)  Eilert Loevborg, listen to

me. Do it – beautifully!

**Loevborg**   Beautifully? (*Smiles.*) With a crown of vine leaves in my hair? The way you used to dream of me – in the old days?

**Hedda**   No. I don't believe in that crown any longer. But – do it beautifully, all the same. Just this once. Goodbye. You must go now. And don't come back.

**Loevborg**   Adieu, madame. Give my love to George Tesman. (*Turns to go.*)

**Hedda**   Wait. I want to give you a souvenir to take with you.

*She goes over to the writing-table, opens the drawer and the pistol-case, and comes back to* **Loevborg** *with one of the pistols.*

**Loevborg** (*looks at her*)   This? Is this the souvenir?

**Hedda** (*nods slowly*)   You recognize it? You looked down its barrel once.

**Loevborg**   You should have used it then.

**Hedda**   Here! Use it now!

**Loevborg** (*puts the pistol in his breast pocket*)   Thank you.

**Hedda**   Do it beautifully, Eilert Loevborg. Only promise me that!

**Loevborg**   Goodbye, Hedda Gabler.

*He goes out through the hall.* **Hedda** *stands by the door for a moment, listening. Then she goes over to the writing-table, takes out the package containing the manuscript, glances inside, pulls some of the pages half out and looks at them. Then she takes it to the armchair by the stove and sits down with the package in her lap. After a moment, she opens the door of the stove; then she opens the packet.*

**Hedda** (*throws one of the pages into the stove and whispers to herself*)   I'm burning your child, Thea! You with your beautiful, wavy hair! (*She throws a few more pages into the stove.*)

The child Eilert Loevborg gave you. (*Throws the rest of the manuscript in.*) I'm burning it! I'm burning your child!

# Act Four

*The same. It is evening. The drawing-room is in darkness. The small room is illuminated by the hanging lamp over the table. The curtains are drawn across the french windows.* **Hedda**, *dressed in black, is walking up and down in the darkened room. Then she goes into the small room and crosses to the left. A few chords are heard from the piano. She comes back into the drawing-room.*

**Bertha** *comes through the small room from the right with a lighted lamp, which she places on the table in front of the corner sofa in the drawing-room. Her eyes are red with crying, and she has black ribbons on her cap. She goes quietly out, right.* **Hedda** *goes over to the french windows, draws the curtains slightly to one side and looks out into the darkness.*

*A few moments later,* **Miss Tesman** *enters from the hall. She is dressed in mourning, with a black hat and veil.* **Hedda** *goes to meet her and holds out her hand.*

**Miss Tesman**  Well, Hedda, here I am in the weeds of sorrow. My poor sister has ended her struggles at last.

**Hedda**  I've already heard. Tesman sent me a card.

**Miss Tesman**  Yes, he promised me he would. But I thought, no, I must go and break the news of death of Hedda myself – here, in the house of life.

**Hedda**  It's very kind of you.

**Miss Tesman**  Ah, Rena shouldn't have chosen a time like this to pass away. This is no moment for Hedda's house to be a place of mourning.

**Hedda** (*changing the subject*)  She died peacefully, Miss Tesman?

**Miss Tesman**  Oh, it was quite beautiful! The end came so calmly. And she was so happy at being able to see George once again. And say goodbye to him. Hasn't he come home yet?

**Hedda**  No. He wrote that I mustn't expect him too soon. But please sit down.

**Miss Tesman**  No, thank you, Hedda dear – bless you. I'd like to. But I've so little time. I must dress her and lay her out as well as I can. She shall go to her grave looking really beautiful.

**Hedda**  Can't I help with anything?

**Miss Tesman**  Why, you mustn't think of such a thing! Hedda Tesman mustn't let her hands be soiled by contact with death. Or her thoughts. Not at this time.

**Hedda**  One can't always control one's thoughts.

**Miss Tesman** (*continues*)  Ah, well, that's life. Now we must start to sew poor Rena's shroud. There'll be sewing to be done in this house, too, before long, I shouldn't wonder. But not for a shroud, praise God.

**George Tesman** *enters from the hall.*

**Hedda**  You've come at least! Thank heavens!

**Tesman**  Are you here, Auntie Juju? With Hedda? Fancy that!

**Miss Tesman**  I was just on the point of leaving, dear boy. Well, have you done everything you promised me?

**Tesman**  No, I'm afraid I forgot half of it. I'll have to run over again tomorrow. My head's in a complete whirl today. I can't collect my thoughts.

**Miss Tesman**  But, George dear, you mustn't take it like this.

**Tesman**  Oh? Well – er – how should I?

**Miss Tesman**  You must be happy in your grief. Happy for what's happened. As I am.

**Tesman**  Oh, yes, yes. You're thinking of Aunt Rena.

**Hedda**  It'll be lonely for you now, Miss Tesman.

**Miss Tesman**   For the first few days, yes. But it won't
last long, I hope. Poor dear Rena's little room isn't going
to stay empty.

**Tesman**   Oh? Whom are you going to move in there?
What?

**Miss Tesman**   Oh, there's always some poor invalid who
needs care and attention.

**Hedda**   Do you really want another cross like that to
bear?

**Miss Tesman**   Cross! God forgive you, child. It's been
no cross for me.

**Hedda**   But now – if a complete stranger comes to live
with you – ?

**Miss Tesman**   Oh, one soon makes friends with invalids.
And I need so much to have someone to live for. Like you,
my dear. Well, I expect there'll soon be work in this house
too for an old aunt, praise God!

**Hedda**   Oh – please!

**Tesman**   My word, yes! What a splendid time the three
of us could have together if –

**Hedda**   If?

**Tesman** (*uneasily*)   Oh, never mind. It'll all work out. Let's
hope so – what?

**Miss Tesman**   Yes, yes. Well, I'm sure you two would
like to be alone. (*Smiles.*) Perhaps Hedda may have
something to tell you, George. Goodbye. I must go home
to Rena. (*Turns to the door.*) Dear God, how strange! Now
Rena is with me and with poor dear Joachim.

**Tesman**   Why, yes, Auntie Juju! What?

**Miss Tesman** *goes out through the hall.*

**Hedda** (*follows* **Tesman** *coldly and searchingly with her eyes*)
I really believe this death distresses you more than it does

her.

**Tesman**   Oh, it isn't just Auntie Rena. It's Eilert I'm so worried about.

**Hedda** (*quickly*)   Is there any news of him?

**Tesman**   I ran over to see him this afternoon. I wanted to tell him his manuscript was in safe hands.

**Hedda**   Oh? You didn't find him?

**Tesman**   No. He wasn't at home. But later I met Mrs Elvsted and she told me he'd been here early this morning.

**Hedda**   Yes, just after you'd left.

**Tesman**   It seems he said he'd torn the manuscript up. What?

**Hedda**   Yes, he claimed to have done so.

**Tesman**   You told him we had it, of course?

**Hedda**   No. (*Quickly.*) Did you tell Mrs Elvsted?

**Tesman**   No, I didn't like to. But you ought to have told him. Think if he should go home and do something desperate! Give me the manuscript, Hedda. I'll run over to him with it right away. Where did you put it?

**Hedda** (*cold and motionless, leaning against the armchair*)   I haven't got it any longer.

**Tesman**   Haven't got it? What on earth do you mean?

**Hedda**   I've burned it.

**Tesman** (*starts, terrified*)   Burned it! Burned Eilert's manuscript.

**Hedda**   Don't shout. The servant will hear you.

**Tesman**   Burned it! But in heaven's name –! Oh, no, no, no! This is impossible!

**Hedda**   Well, it's true.

**Tesman**   But, Hedda, do you realize what you've done?

That's appropriating lost property! It's against the law! By God! You ask Judge Brack and see if I'm not right.

**Hedda**   You'd be well advised not to talk about it to Judge Brack or anyone else.

**Tesman**   But how could you go and do such a dreadful thing? What on earth put the idea into your head? What came over you? Answer me! What?

**Hedda** (*represses an almost imperceptible smile*)   I did it for your sake, George.

**Tesman**   For my sake?

**Hedda**   When you came home this morning and described how he'd read his book to you –

**Tesman**   Yes, yes?

**Hedda**   You admitted you were jealous of him.

**Tesman**   But, good heavens, I didn't mean it literally!

**Hedda**   No matter. I couldn't bear the thought that anyone else should push you into the background.

**Tesman** (*torn between doubt and joy*)   Hedda – is this true? But – but – but I never realized you loved me like that! Fancy that!

**Hedda**   Well, I suppose you'd better know. I'm going to have – (*Breaks off and says violently.*) No, no – you'd better ask your Auntie Juju. She'll tell you.

**Tesman**   Hedda! I think I understand what you mean. (*Clasps his hands.*) Good heavens, can it really be true? What?

**Hedda**   Don't shout. The servant will hear you.

**Tesman** (*laughing with joy*)   The servant! I say, that's good! The servant! Why, that's Bertha! I'll run out and tell her at once!

**Hedda** (*clenches her hands in despair*)   Oh, it's destroying me, all this – it's destroying me!

**Tesman**   I say, Hedda, what's up? What?

**Hedda** (*cold, controlled*)   Oh, it's all so – absurd – George.

**Tesman**   Absurd? That I'm so happy? But surely – ? Ah, well – perhaps I won't say anything to Bertha.

**Hedda**   No, do. She might as well know, too.

**Tesman**   No, no, I won't tell her yet. But Auntie Juju – I must let her know! And you – you called me George! For the first time! Fancy that! Oh, it'll make Auntie Juju so happy, all this! So very happy!

**Hedda**   Will she be happy when she heard I've burned Eilert Loevborg's manuscript – for your sake?

**Tesman**   No, I'd forgotten about that. Of course, no one must be allowed to know about the manuscript. But that you're burning with love for me, Hedda, I must certainly let Auntie Juju know that. I say, I wonder if young wives often feel like that towards their husbands? What?

**Hedda**   You might ask Auntie Juju about that, too.

**Tesman**   I will, as soon as I get the chance. (*Looks uneasy and thoughtful again.*) But I say, you know, that manuscript. Dreadful business. Poor Eilert!

**Mrs Elvsted**, *dressed as on her first visit, with hat and overcoat, enters from the hall.*

**Mrs Elvsted** (*greets them hastily and tremulously*)   Oh, Hedda dear, do please forgive me for coming here again.

**Hedda**   Why, Thea, what's happened?

**Tesman**   Is it anything to do with Eilert Loevborg? What?

**Mrs Elvsted**   Yes – I'm so dreadfully afraid he may have met with an accident.

**Hedda** (*grips her arm*)   You think so?

**Tesman**   But, good heavens, Mrs Elvsted, what makes you think that?

**Mrs Elvsted**  I heard them talking about him at the boarding-house, as I went in. Oh, there are the most terrible rumours being spread about him in town today.

**Tesman**  Er – yes, I heard about them, too. But I can testify that he went straight home to bed. Fancy – !

**Hedda**  Well – what did they say in the boarding-house?

**Mrs Elvsted**  Oh, I couldn't find out anything. Either they didn't know, or else – They stopped talking when they saw me. And I didn't dare to ask.

**Tesman**  (*fidgets uneasily*)  We must hope – we must hope you misheard them, Mrs Elvsted.

**Mrs Elvsted**  No, no, I'm sure it was him they were talking about. I heard them say something about a hospital –

**Tesman**  Hospital!

**Hedda**  Oh no, surely that's impossible!

**Mrs Elvsted**  Oh, I became so afraid. So I went up to his rooms and asked to see him.

**Hedda**  Do you think that was wise, Thea?

**Mrs Elvsted**  Well, what else could I do? I couldn't bear the uncertainty any longer.

**Tesman**  But *you* didn't manage to find him either? What?

**Mrs Elvsted**  No. And they had no idea where he was. They said he hadn't been home since yesterday afternoon.

**Tesman**  Since yesterday? Fancy that!

**Mrs Elvsted**  I'm sure he must have met with an accident.

**Tesman**  Hedda, I wonder if I ought to go into town and make one or two enquiries?

**Hedda**  No, no, don't you get mixed up in this.

**Judge Brack** *enters from the hall, hat in hand.* **Bertha**, *who has opened the door for him, closes it. He looks serious and greets them silently.*

**Tesman**   Hullo, my dear Judge. Fancy seeing you!

**Brack**   I had to come and talk to you.

**Tesman**   I can see Auntie Juju's told you the news.

**Brack**   Yes, I've heard about that, too.

**Tesman**   Tragic, isn't it?

**Brack**   Well, my dear chap, that depends how you look at it.

**Tesman** *(looks uncertainly at him)*   Has something else happened?

**Brack**   Yes.

**Hedda**   Another tragedy?

**Brack**   That also depends on how you look at it, Mrs Tesman.

**Mrs Elvsted**   Oh, it's something to do with Eilert Loevborg!

**Brack** *(looks at her for a moment)*   How did you guess? Perhaps you've heard already – ?

**Mrs Elvsted** *(confused)*   No, no, not at all – I –

**Tesman**   For heaven's sake, tell us!

**Brack** *(shrugs his shoulders)*   Well, I'm afraid they've taken him to the hospital. He's dying.

**Mrs Elvsted** *(screams)*   Oh God, God!

**Tesman**   The hospital! Dying!

**Hedda** *(involuntarily)*   So quickly!

**Mrs Elvsted** *(weeping)*   Oh, Hedda! And we parted enemies!

**Hedda** (*whispers*)   Thea – Thea!

**Mrs Elvsted** (*ignoring her*)   I must see him! I must see him before he dies!

**Brack**   It's no use, Mrs Elvsted. No one's allowed to see him now.

**Mrs Elvsted**   But what's happened to him? You must tell me!

**Tesman**   He hasn't tried to do anything to himself? What?

**Hedda**   Yes, he has. I'm sure of it.

**Tesman**   Hedda, how can you – ?

**Brack** (*who has not taken his eyes from her*)   I'm afraid you've guessed correctly, Mrs Tesman.

**Mrs Elvsted**   How dreadful!

**Tesman**   Attempted suicide! Fancy that!

**Hedda**   Shot himself!

**Brack**   Right again, Mrs Tesman.

**Mrs Elvsted** (*tries to compose herself*)   When did this happen, Judge Brack?

**Brack**   This afternoon. Between three and four.

**Tesman**   But, good heavens – where? What?

**Brack** (*a little hesitantly*)   Where? Why, my dear chap, in his rooms, of course.

**Mrs Elvsted**   No, that's impossible. I was there soon after six.

**Brack**   Well, it must have been somewhere else, then. I don't know exactly. I only know that they found him. He's shot himself – through the breast.

**Mrs Elvsted**   Oh, how horrible! That he should end like that!

**Hedda** (*to* **Brack**)   Through the breast, you said?

**Brack**   That is what I said.

**Hedda**   Not through the head?

**Brack**   Through the breast, Mrs Tesman.

**Hedda**   The breast. Yes; yes. That's good, too.

**Brack**   Why, Mrs Tesman?

**Hedda**   Oh – no, I didn't mean anything.

**Tesman**   And the wound's dangerous, you say? What?

**Brack**   Mortal. He's probably already dead.

**Mrs Elvsted**   Yes, yes – I feel it! It's all over. All over. Oh Hedda – !

**Tesman**   But, tell me, how did you manage to learn all this?

**Brack** (*curtly*)   From the police. I spoke to one of them.

**Hedda** (*loudly, clearly*)   Thank God! At last!

**Tesman** (*appalled*)   For God's sake, Hedda, what are you saying?

**Hedda**   I am saying there's beauty in what he has done.

**Brack**   Hm – Mrs Tesman –

**Tesman**   Beauty! Oh, but I say!

**Mrs Elvsted**   Hedda, how can you talk of beauty in connexion with a thing like this?

**Hedda**   Eilert Loevborg has settled his account with life. He's had the courage to do what – what he had to do.

**Mrs Elvsted**   No, that's not why it happened. He did it because he was mad.

**Tesman**   He did it because he was desperate.

**Hedda**   You're wrong! I know!

**Mrs Elvsted**   He must have been mad. The same as when he tore up the manuscript.

**Brack** (*starts*)   Manuscript? Did he tear it up?

**Mrs Elvsted**   Yes. Last night.

**Tesman** (*whispers*)   Oh, Hedda, we shall never be able to escape from this.

**Brack**   Hm. Strange.

**Tesman** (*wanders round the room*)   To think of Eilert dying like that. And not leaving behind him the thing that would have made his name endure.

**Mrs Elvsted**   If only it could be pieced together again!

**Tesman**   Yes, yes, yes! If only it could! I'd give anything –

**Mrs Elvsted**   Perhaps it can, Mr Tesman.

**Tesman**   What do you mean?

**Mrs Elvsted** (*searches in the pocket of her dress*)   Look. I kept the notes he dictated it from.

**Hedda** (*takes a step nearer*)   Ah!

**Tesman**   You kept them, Mrs Elvsted! What?

**Mrs Elvsted**   Yes, here they are. I brought them with me when I left home. They've been in my pocket ever since.

**Tesman**   Let me have a look.

**Mrs Elvsted** (*hands him a wad of small sheets of paper*)   They're in a terrible muddle. All mixed up.

**Tesman**   I say, just fancy if we could sort them out! Perhaps if we work on them together – ?

**Mrs Elvsted**   Oh, yes! Let's try, anyway!

**Tesman**   We'll manage it. We must! I shall dedicate my life to this.

**Hedda**   *You*, George? Your life?

**Tesman**   Yes – well, all the time I can spare. My book'll have to wait. Hedda, you do understand? What? I owe it to Eilert's memory.

**Hedda**   Perhaps.

**Tesman**   Well, my dear Mrs Elvsted, you and I'll have to pool our brains. No use crying over spilt milk, what? We must try to approach this matter calmly.

**Mrs Elvsted**   Yes, yes, Mr Tesman. I'll do my best.

**Tesman**   Well, come over here and let's start looking at these notes right away. Where shall we sit? Here? No, the other room. You'll excuse us, won't you, Judge? Come along with me, Mrs Elvsted.

**Mrs Elvsted**   Oh, God! If only we can manage to do it!

**Tesman** *and* **Mrs Elvsted** *go into the rear room. He takes off his hat and overcoat. They sit at the table beneath the hanging lamp and absorb themselves in the notes.* **Hedda** *walks across to the stove and sits in the armchair. After a moment,* **Brack** *goes over to her.*

**Hedda** (*half aloud*)   Oh, Judge! This act of Eilert Loevborg's – doesn't it give one a sense of release!

**Brack**   Release, Mrs Hedda? Well, it's a release for him, of course –

**Hedda**   Oh, I don't mean him – I mean me! The release of knowing that someone can do something really brave! Something beautiful!

**Brack** (*smiles*)   Hm – my dear Mrs Hedda –

**Hedda**   Oh, I know what you're going to say. You're a *bourgeois* at heart, too, just like – ah, well!

**Brack** (*looks at her*)   Eilert Loevborg has meant more to you than you're willing to admit to yourself. Or am I wrong?

**Hedda**   I'm not answering questions like that from you. I

only know that Eilert Loevborg has had the courage to live according to his own principles. And now, at last, he's done something big! Something beautiful! To have the courage and the will to rise from the feast of life so early!

**Brack**   It distresses me deeply, Mrs Hedda, but I'm afraid I must rob you of that charming illusion.

**Hedda**   Illusion?

**Brack**   You wouldn't have been allowed to keep it for long, anyway.

**Hedda**   What do you mean?

**Brack**   He didn't shoot himself on purpose.

**Hedda**   Not on purpose?

**Brack**   No. It didn't happen quite the way I told you.

**Hedda**   Have you been hiding something? What is it?

**Brack**   In order to spare poor Mrs Elvsted's feelings, I permitted myself one or two small – equivocations.

**Hedda**   What?

**Brack**   To begin with, he is already dead.

**Hedda**   He died at the hospital?

**Brack**   Yes. Without regaining consciousness.

**Hedda**   What else haven't you told us?

**Brack**   The incident didn't take place at his lodgings.

**Hedda**   Well, that's utterly unimportant.

**Brack**   Not utterly. The fact is, you see, that Eilert Loevborg was found shot in Mademoiselle Danielle's boudoir.

**Hedda**   (*almost jumps up, but instead sinks back in her chair*) That's impossible. He can't have been there today.

**Brack**   He was there this afternoon. He went to ask for something he claimed they'd taken from him. Talked some

crazy nonsense about a child which had got lost –

**Hedda**   Oh! So that was the reason!

**Brack**   I thought at first he might have been referring to his manuscript. But I fear he destroyed that himself. So he must have meant his pocket-book – I suppose.

**Hedda**   Yes, I suppose so. So they found him there?

**Brack**   Yes; there. With a discharged pistol in his breast pocket. The shot had wounded him mortally.

**Hedda**   Yes. In the breast.

**Brack**   No. In the – stomach. The – lower part –

**Hedda** (*looks at him with an expression of repulsion*)   That, too! Oh, why does everything I touch become mean and ludicrous? It's like a curse!

**Brack**   There's something else, Mrs Hedda. It's rather disagreeable, too.

**Hedda**   What?

**Brack**   The pistol he had on him –

**Hedda**   Yes? What about it?

**Brack**   He must have stolen it.

**Hedda** (*jumps up*)   Stolen it! That isn't true! He didn't!

**Brack**   It's the only explanation. He must have stolen it. Ssh!

**Tesman** and **Mrs Elvsted** *have got up from the table in the rear room and come into the drawing-room.*

**Tesman** (*his hands full of papers*)   Hedda, I can't see properly under that lamp. Do you think – ?

**Hedda**   I am thinking.

**Tesman**   Do you think we could possibly use your writing-table for a little? What?

**Hedda**   Yes, of course. (*Quickly.*) No, wait! Let me tidy it

up first.

**Tesman**  Oh, don't you trouble about that. There's plenty of room.

**Hedda**  No, no, let me tidy it up first, I say. I'll take these in and put them on the piano. Here.

*She pulls an object, covered with sheets of music, out from under the bookcase, puts some more sheets on top and carries it all into the rear room and away to the left.* **Tesman** *puts his papers on the writing-table and moves the lamp over from the corner table. He and* **Mrs Elvsted** *sit down and begin working again.* **Hedda** *comes back.*

(*Behind* **Mrs Elvsted**'s *chair, ruffles her hair gently.*) Well, my pretty Thea. And how is work progressing on Eilert Loevborg's memorial?

**Mrs Elvsted** (*looks up at her, dejectedly*)  Oh, it's going to be terribly difficult to get these into any order.

**Tesman**  We've got to do it. We must! After all, putting other people's papers into order is rather my speciality, what?

**Hedda** *goes over to the stove and sits on one of the footstools.* **Brack** *stands over her, leaning against the armchair.*

**Hedda** (*whispers*)  What was that you were saying about the pistol?

**Brack** (*softly*)  I said he must have stolen it.

**Hedda**  Why do you think that?

**Brack**  Because any other explanation is unthinkable, Mrs Hedda. Or ought to be.

**Hedda**  I see.

**Brack** (*looks at her for a moment*)  Eilert Loevborg was here this morning. Wasn't he?

**Hedda**  Yes.

**Brack**  Were you alone with him?

**Hedda**   For a few moments.

**Brack**   You didn't leave the room while he was here?

**Hedda**   No.

**Brack**   Think again. Are you sure you didn't go out for a moment?

**Hedda**   Oh – yes, I might have gone into the hall. Just for a few seconds.

**Brack**   And where was your pistol-case during this time?

**Hedda**   I'd locked it in that –

**Brack**   Er – Mrs Hedda?

**Hedda**   It was lying over there on my writing-table.

**Brack**   Have you looked to see if both the pistols are still there?

**Hedda**   No.

**Brack**   You needn't bother. I saw the pistol Loevborg had when they found him. I recognized it at once. From yesterday. And other occasions.

**Hedda**   Have you got it?

**Brack**   No. The police have it.

**Hedda**   What will the police do with this pistol?

**Brack**   Try to trace the owner.

**Hedda**   Do you think they'll succeed?

**Brack** (*leans down and whispers*)   No, Hedda Gabler. Not as long as I hold my tongue.

**Hedda** (*looks nervously at him*)   And if you don't?

**Brack** (*shrugs his shoulders*)   You could always say he'd stolen it.

**Hedda**   I'd rather die!

**Brack** (*smiles*)   People say that. They never do it.

**Hedda** (*not replying*)   And suppose the pistol wasn't stolen? And they trace the owner? What then?

**Brack**   There'll be a scandal, Hedda.

**Hedda**   A scandal!

**Brack**   Yes, a scandal. The thing you're so frightened of. You'll have to appear in court together with Mademoiselle Danielle. She'll have to explain how it all happened. Was it an accident, or was it – homicide? Was he about to take the pistol from his pocket to threaten her? And did it go off? Or did she snatch the pistol from his hand, shoot him and then put it back in his pocket? She might easily have done it. She's a resourceful lady, is Mademoiselle Danielle.

**Hedda**   But I have nothing to do with this repulsive business.

**Brack**   No. But you'll have to answer one question. Why did you give Eilert Loevborg this pistol? And what conclusions will people draw when it is proved you did give it to him?

**Hedda** (*bows her head*)   That's true. I hadn't thought of that.

**Brack**   Well, luckily there's no danger as long as I hold my tongue.

**Hedda** (*looks up at him*)   In other words, I'm in your power, Judge. From now on, you've got your hold over me.

**Brack** (*whispers, more slowly*)   Hedda, my dearest – believe me – I will not abuse my position.

**Hedda**   Nevertheless, I'm in your power. Dependent on your will, and your demands. Not free. Still not free! (*Rises passionately.*) No. I couldn't bear that. No.

**Brack** (*looks half-derisively at her*)   Most people resign themselves to the inevitable, sooner or later.

**Hedda** (*returns his gaze*)   Possibly they do.

*She goes across to the writing-table.*

(*Represses an involuntary smile and says in* **Tesman**'s *voice.*) Well, George. Think you'll be able to manage? What?

**Tesman** Heaven knows, dear. This is going to take months and months.

**Hedda** (*in the same tone as before*) Fancy that, by Jove! (*Runs her hands gently through* **Mrs Elvsted**'s *hair.*) Doesn't it feel strange, Thea? Here you are working away with Tesman just the way you used to work with Eilert Loevborg.

**Mrs Elvsted** Oh – if only I can inspire your husband, too!

**Hedda** Oh, it'll come. In time.

**Tesman** Yes – do you know, Hedda, I really think I'm beginning to feel a bit – well – that way. But you go back and talk to Judge Brack.

**Hedda** Can't I be of use to you two in any way?

**Tesman** No, none at all. (*Turns his head.*) You'll have to keep Hedda company from now on, Judge, and see she doesn't get bored. If you don't mind.

**Brack** (*glances at* **Hedda**) It'll be a pleasure.

**Hedda** Thank you. But I'm tired this evening. I think I'll lie down on the sofa in there for a little while.

**Tesman** Yes, dear – do. What?

**Hedda** *goes into the rear room and draws the curtains behind her. Short pause. Suddenly she begins to play a frenzied dance melody on the piano.*

**Mrs Elvsted** (*starts up from her chair*) Oh, what's that?

**Tesman** (*runs to the doorway*) Hedda dear, please! Don't play dance music tonight! Think of Auntie Rena. And Eilert.

**Hedda** (*puts her head through the curtains*) And Auntie Juju. And all the rest of them. From now on I'll be quiet.

*She closes the curtains behind her.*

**Tesman** (*at the writing-table*)   It distresses her to watch us doing this. I say, Mrs Elvsted, I've an idea. Why don't you move in with Auntie Juju? I'll run over each evening, and we can sit and work there. What?

**Mrs Elvsted**   Yes, that might be the best plan.

**Hedda** (*from the rear room*)   I can hear what you're saying, Tesman. But how shall I spend the evenings out here?

*nailed → the coffin*

**Tesman** (*looking through his papers*)   Oh, I'm sure Judge Brack'll be kind enough to come over and keep you company. You won't mind my not being here, Judge?

**Brack** (*in the armchair, calls gaily*)   I'll be delighted, Mrs Tesman. I'll be here every evening. We'll have great fun together, you and I.

**Hedda** (*loud and clear*)   Yes, that'll suit you, won't it, Judge? The only cock on the dunghill –

*A shot is heard from the rear room.* **Tesman**, **Mrs Elvsted** *and* **Judge Brack** *start from their chairs.*

**Tesman**   Oh, she's playing with those pistols again.

*He pulls the curtains aside and runs in.* **Mrs Elvsted** *follows him.* **Hedda** *is lying dead on the sofa. Confusion and shouting.* **Bertha** *enters in alarm from the right.*

**Tesman** (*screams to* **Brack**)   She's shot herself! Shot herself in the head! Fancy that!

**Brack** (*half paralysed in the armchair*)   But, good God! People don't do such things!

*tragic idiosyncrasy*

*underestimated her*
*as is her ?*

*courageous – in self refer to herself saying she's a coward.*

*people don't do such thing?*

*female power in male dominant society.*

*Hedda's*

# Note on the Translation

The main problem in translating *Hedda Gabler* is to contrast
the snobbish and consciously upper-class speech of Hedda
and Judge Brack with the naïve and homely way of talking
shared by Miss Tesman, Bertha and George Tesman.
Hedda is a general's daughter and lets no one forget it.
George Tesman has unconsciously acquired the nanny-like
mode of speech of the old aunts who brought him up. He
addresses Aunt Juliana as *Tante Julle*, a particularly irritating
and baby-like abbreviation which drives Hedda mad every
time he uses it. The last straw is when he asks her to
address the old lady by it, too. To render this as Auntie
Julie, as has usually been done, is completely to miss the
point; it must be a ridiculous nickname such as Juju. When
Brack tells Hedda where Loevborg has shot himself, he
must make it clear to her that the bullet destroyed his
sexual organs; otherwise Hedda's reactions make no sense.
To translate this as 'belly' or 'bowels' is again to miss the
point, yet Brack must not use the phrase 'sexual organs'
directly; he is far too subtle a campaigner to speak so
bluntly to a lady. What he says is: 'In the – stomach. The
– lower part.' I have altered the name of the red-haired
singer from Mademoiselle Diana, which is difficult to say in
English and has an improbable ring about it, to
Mademoiselle Danielle.

In the Norwegian, Hedda addresses her husband as
Tesman except on the crucial occasions at the end of Act 1
and in Act 4, when she deliberately switches to his
Christian name. Similarly, Brack calls Hedda Mrs Tesman
when anyone else is present, but Mrs Hedda when they are
alone together; only towards the very end of the play does
he address her simply as Hedda. Although this usage is un-
English, even for the period, it is, in fact, effective on the
stage when one has the illusion of eavesdropping on a
foreign nineteenth-century family, and I have let it stand.
To allow Brack to call her Hedda the first time we see
them alone together in Act 2 suggests an intimacy which
they have not yet reached.

# Notes

*Act One*

lxxxii  *research graduate*:  George Tesman's status is that of a Research Fellow.

7  *two empty rooms*:  these are intended as nurseries, but George is too slow on the uptake to realise this.

9  *Eilert Loevborg*:  Tesman's main rival in the field of cultural history. Although wayward, he is very gifted. While Tesman's key research project is focused on the domestic industries of Brabant in the Middle Ages, Loevborg has just published a brilliant new work on the history of civilisation.

13  *filled out*:  Auntie Juju recovers swiftly from Hedda's deliberate insult at the mention of Hedda having filled out, which she takes to mean that Hedda is pregnant.

18  *regular in his habits*:  Eilert had a severe drink problem in the past and was a regular client at Mademoiselle Danielle's brothel. These are hardly ideal recommendations for someone who is to tutor young children.

26  *she tried to shoot him*:  we later discover that it was Hedda herself, not Mademoiselle Danielle (the red-headed singer), who once threatened to shoot Eilert.

28  *Hedda sighs*:  Ibsen doesn't specify a sigh here, but the suggestion is entirely justified. Hedda finds Tesman's behaviour, including his inability to remember names, completely exasperating.

31  *You must be prepared for your nomination ...*:  what is implied here is that the appointing committee for the Chair in Cultural History had been taking soundings and had already indicated to George that he would be offered the Chair.

33  *George darling*:  Hedda normally addresses Tesman

by his surname. Here she calls him by his first
name in a way that is deliberately ironic. The
translator adds the word 'darling' to emphasise the
intended ironic tone.

*Act Two*

35 *dressed for a bachelor party*:   i.e. in evening dress (white
tie and tails).

37 *one of us*:   the reference establishes the fact that
Hedda and Brack regard themselves as belonging to
a totally different class from Tesman and his aunties.

43 *the late Prime Minister's house*:   the fact that the house
belonged to the late Prime Minister and then to his
window confirms its status as a property of some
importance.

45 *the most solemn of human responsibilities*:   Brack is
referring to Hedda's possible pregnancy and probes
her attitude to motherhood.

47 *do you think it'll be all right for him to stay here with
you?*:   Tesman is not keen on the prospect of
leaving Hedda alone with Eilert. But at the end of
the play he is perfectly willing for Judge Brack to
keep her company while he works at Auntie Juju's
on the notes for Eilert's manuscript.

48 *We – met some years ago*:   Brack's distinctly hesitant
comment that he and Eilert met some years ago
might imply that Eilert appeared before him in
court after one of his drunken escapades.

49 *this is about the future*:   Eilert's new book, which only
exists in manuscript form, deals with those forces
that will shape our civilisation and indicates the
direction in which that civilisation may develop.
This places it firmly within the framework of
naturalist thinking that had developed since the
late 1860s. For instance, the French aesthetic
philosopher, Hippolyte Taine, had identified three
key forces that shape civilisation in his *Introduction to
English Literature* (1863): these were *la race* (race), *le*

*milieu* (surroundings), *le moment* (epoch). Taine
argued that, if the effects of these forces could be
properly measured, as was the case with other
mechanical forces, this would enable the future
development of civilisation to be predicted.

54 *this little village*:   the village down by the Brenner
Pass is Gossensass (Colle Isarco), which had
important associations for Ibsen as well as Hedda.
The implication of Hedda's comment, 'and met all
those amusing people', is that she may have enjoyed
herself sufficiently at Gossensass to be persuaded to
sleep with Tesman. This makes his next comment
all the more incongruous, 'if only we could have
had you with us, Eilert!'

57 *Take care! Don't you delude yourself!*:   in Bergman's
London production, after Hedda's confession, Robert
Stephens (who played Loevborg) made another
physical pass at Hedda, which immediately provokes
this comment.

58 *We're just good friends*:   Loevborg denies that there is
any physical dimension to his relationship with
Thea. This fits with the ideas of companionship
between men and women that Ibsen had expressed
in his notes for the play. If true, it also confirms
that Thea is risking her reputation as a married
woman for the sake of companionship rather than
because of a conventional extra-marital affair.

64 *With a crown of vine leaves in his hair!*:   the notion of
a crown of vine leaves in Loevborg's hair is an
image that Ibsen had already used in his earlier
philosophical work *Emperor and Galilean*. The
Emperor Julian, torn between the conflicting
demands of paganism and Christianity, embraces a
pagan ideal of beauty. For him this is summed up
in an image of Dionysian youths dancing with vine
leaves in their hair. However, the undue emphasis
he places on pagan beauty leads to a disastrous
conflict with the forces of Christianity in which he is

eventually killed. In articulating this image of
Loevborg with vine leaves in his hair, Hedda
embraces a pagan ideal of Dionysian beauty that
will lead to an equally disastrous outcome. As in the
earlier play, the conflict between an essentially
pagan desire for beauty, pursued with a destructive
lack of balance, and the demands of a Christian
moral order results in the leading character being
crushed by the forces of historical inevitability.

## Act Three

69 *less afraid of life than most men*:  Hedda's fascination
with the image of Dionysian beauty is confirmed
here. She goes on to enquire almost naively whether
Loevborg had vine leaves in his hair.

75 *Mademoiselle Danielle*:  in Ibsen's text, the 'sporting
establishment' (or brothel) belongs to Mademoiselle
Diana. The translator changed the name to Danielle
because he felt the name sounded more natural in
English. However, in so doing he lost the parallel
with the mythical goddess of the chase. Ibsen also
uses the name of Diana ironically, as Diana, almost
uniquely amongst the gods, represented virtue and
chastity.

81 *But that's not – !*:  Hedda could easily intervene here
to return Loevborg's manuscript. But she is made
even more jealous than before by Thea referring to
the manuscript as a child, her child with Loevborg.
It is probably at this moment that Hedda conceives
the idea, fuelled by her jealousy, to burn Thea's
child, i.e. the manuscript.

84 *Do it beautifully*:  Hedda asks Loevborg to shoot
himself beautifully. His ironic reply makes it clear
that she has long dreamt of Loevborg as a liberated
Dionysian. Even in the old days she harboured
fantasy images of him with a crown of vine leaves
in his hair.

*Act Four*

90 *George*:   for the second time in the play, Hedda uses
Tesman's first name. However, this time she is not
being ironic. She is pretending to be affectionate, as
she tells George of her pregnancy. Even now,
however, the mask slips very rapidly and her real
feelings show through with disturbing clarity.

95 *there's beauty in what he has done*:   before Hedda learns
the whole truth about Eilert's suicide, she still clings
to her fantasy notion of pagan beauty. Eilert is a
true pagan who has killed himself beautifully.

99 *In the – stomach. The – lower part*:   Brack soon
disabuses Hedda of her pagan idealism. In
Bergman's London production, John Moffatt (who
played Brack) pointed towards his crotch as he said
this. Instead of dying beautifully, Loevborg died
from an accidental shot to the genitals while
quarrelling in a brothel.

# Questions for Further Study

1. Explore some of the reasons why Hedda decided to marry Tesman. What kind of relationship does she have with her husband and his aunts?

2. Describe the nature of Hedda's past relationship with Loevborg. Why does she view her past response to him as cowardly?

3. Compare Hedda and Thea as characters, outlining their contrasting motives for action and the way they relate to other people.

4. Why does Hedda find Judge Brack both entertaining and threatening? Comment on their different views of relationships between the sexes.

5. Analyse some of the ways in which class differences underpin the action of *Hedda Gabler*.

6. How far do you agree that the action of *Hedda Gabler* revolves primarily around money, social status and sex?

7. Some critics have commented that Hedda Gabler is too complex a character for a stage play. Argue for or against this view.

8. If you were directing a production of *Hedda Gabler*, what advice would you give to the actress playing the title role to help her firstly understand the complexity of Hedda's responses and then find an appropriate style to convey this complexity?

9. In what ways do the linear structure of the play and the taut, compressed dialogue influence the overall tone and mood of the play?

10. Explore the tension between comic and serious effects in the action and dialogue of the play.

11. In what ways are visual and non-verbal features used to communicate meaning in the play?

12. Analyse ways that the use of stage space in the play communicates insights into the characters' hidden thoughts and intentions.

13. Explore some of the subtextual meanings attached to General Gabler's pistols. In what ways do these meanings affect the use of the pistols in the action of the play?

14. How do environmental pressures affect the behaviour of two or more characters in *Hedda Gabler*?

15. In what ways has Hedda's upbringing as a widowed general's daughter proved to be socially and psychologically disabling? What freedom of action is left to her as an adult?

16. Choosing any two characters in the play, compare behaviour that seems a product of determinism with behaviour that seems to suggest that people can act freely and responsibly.

17. How far does *Hedda Gabler* adhere to the kind of naturalist demands set out by Zola in his essay 'Naturalism in the Theatre'?

18. Ibsen wrote, 'With Hedda, there is poetry deep down'. How is this expressed in the play?

19. In *Hedda Gabler* some striking visual and atmospheric images are used in the dialogue and in the stage directions. What is their function?

20. In what ways does *Hedda Gabler* challenge the value structures of late nineteenth-century bourgeois society?

21. In what ways does *Hedda Gabler* offer a critique of marriage and the status of women in the society of the day?

22. 'Ibsen's plays invite audiences to make judgements about the behaviour of his characters.' How far is this true of *Hedda Gabler*?

DAVID THOMAS was Professor and Chairman of Theatre Studies at the University of Warwick until his retirement in 2004. He is now a Professor Emeritus at Warwick. He has directed productions of plays by Ibsen, Strindberg, Dryden and Etherege and operas by Strauss, Donizetti, Mozart and Gluck. He has contributed to television programmes on Handel opera (*South Bank Show*) and the Drury Lane playhouse (Channel 4: *Lost Buildings of Britain*). His main publications include: *Henrik Ibsen* (Macmillan, 1983); *Theatre in Europe: A Documentary History. Restoration and Georgian England 1660–1788* (Cambridge University Press, 1989); and *William Congreve* (Macmillan, 1992). More recent publications include a video, *The Restoration Stage: from Tennis Court to Playhouse* (University of Warwick and Films for the Humanities, 1996), and two anthologies of plays, *Six Restoration and French Neoclassic Plays* and *Four Georgian and Pre-Revolutionary Plays* (Macmillan, 1998).

## Methuen Drama Student Editions

Jean Anouilh *Antigone* • John Arden *Serjeant Musgrave's Dance*
Alan Ayckbourn *Confusions* • Aphra Behn *The Rover*
Edward Bond *Lear* • Bertolt Brecht *The Caucasian Chalk Circle*
*Life of Galileo* • *Mother Courage and her Children*
*The Resistible Rise of Arturo Ui* • *The Threepenny Opera*
Anton Chekhov *The Cherry Orchard* • *The Seagull* • *Three Sisters*
*Uncle Vanya* • Caryl Churchill *Serious Money* • *Top Girls*
Shelagh Delaney *A Taste of Honey* • Euripides *Elektra* • *Medea*
Dario Fo *Accidental Death of an Anarchist* • Michael Frayn *Copenhagen*
John Galsworthy *Strife* • Nikolai Gogol *The Government Inspector*
Robert Holman *Across Oka* • Henrik Ibsen *A Doll's House* • *Ghosts*
*Hedda Gabler* • Charlotte Keatley *My Mother Said I Never Should*
Bernard Kops *Dreams of Anne Frank* • Federico García Lorca
*Blood Wedding* • *Doña Rosita the Spinster* (bilingual edition) •*The House
of Bernarda Alba* • (bilingual edition) • *Yerma* (bilingual edition) • David
Mamet *Glengarry Glen Ross* • *Oleanna* • Patrick Marber *Closer* • John
Marston *The Malcontent* • Joe Orton *Loot* • Luigi Pirandello *Six
Characters in Search of an Author* • Mark Ravenhill *Shopping and
F\*\*\*ing* • Willy Russell *Blood Brothers* • *Educating Rita* • Sophocles
*Antigone* • *Oedipus the King* • Wole Soyinka *Death and the King's
Horseman* • August Strindberg *Miss Julie* • J. M. Synge *The Playboy
of the Western World* • Theatre Workshop *Oh What a Lovely War*
Timberlake Wertenbaker *Our Country's Good* • Arnold Wesker *The
Merchant* • Oscar Wilde *The Importance of Being Earnest* • Tennessee
Williams *A Streetcar Named Desire* • *The Glass Menagerie*

# Methuen Drama World Classics

*include*

Jean Anouilh (two volumes)
Brendan Behan
Aphra Behn
Bertolt Brecht (eight volumes)
Büchner
Bulgakov
Calderón
Čapek
Anton Chekhov
Noël Coward (eight volumes)
Feydeau
Eduardo De Filippo
Max Frisch
John Galsworthy
Gogol
Gorky (two volumes)
Harley Granville Barker
  (two volumes)
Victor Hugo
Henrik Ibsen (six volumes)
Jarry

Lorca (three volumes)
Marivaux
Mustapha Matura
David Mercer (two volumes)
Arthur Miller (five volumes)
Molière
Musset
Peter Nichols (two volumes)
Joe Orton
A. W. Pinero
Luigi Pirandello
Terence Rattigan
  (two volumes)
W. Somerset Maugham
  (two volumes)
August Strindberg
  (three volumes)
J. M. Synge
Ramón del Valle-Inclán
Frank Wedekind
Oscar Wilde

# Methuen Drama Contemporary Dramatists

*include*

John Arden (two volumes)
Arden & D'Arcy
Peter Barnes (three volumes)
Sebastian Barry
Dermot Bolger
Edward Bond (eight volumes)
Howard Brenton
  (two volumes)
Richard Cameron
Jim Cartwright
Caryl Churchill (two volumes)
Sarah Daniels (two volumes)
Nick Darke
David Edgar (three volumes)
David Eldridge
Ben Elton
Dario Fo (two volumes)
Michael Frayn (three volumes)
John Godber (three volumes)
Paul Godfrey
David Greig
John Guare
Lee Hall (two volumes)
Peter Handke
Jonathan Harvey
  (two volumes)
Declan Hughes
Terry Johnson (three volumes)
Sarah Kane
Barrie Keefe
Bernard-Marie Koltès
  (two volumes)
Franz Xaver Kroetz
David Lan
Bryony Lavery
Deborah Levy
Doug Lucie

David Mamet (four volumes)
Martin McDonagh
Duncan McLean
Anthony Minghella
  (two volumes)
Tom Murphy (five volumes)
Phyllis Nagy
Anthony Neilson
Philip Osment
Gary Owen
Louise Page
Stewart Parker (two volumes)
Joe Penhall
Stephen Poliakoff
  (three volumes)
David Rabe
Mark Ravenhill
Christina Reid
Philip Ridley
Willy Russell
Eric-Emmanuel Schmitt
Ntozake Shange
Sam Shepard (two volumes)
Wole Soyinka (two volumes)
Simon Stephens
Shelagh Stephenson
David Storey (three volumes)
Sue Townsend
Judy Upton
Michel Vinaver
  (two volumes)
Arnold Wesker (two volumes)
Michael Wilcox
Roy Williams (two volumes)
Snoo Wilson (two volumes)
David Wood (two volumes)
Victoria Wood

# Methuen Drama Modern Plays

*include work by*

Edward Albee
Jean Anouilh
John Arden
Margaretta D'Arcy
Peter Barnes
Sebastian Barry
Brendan Behan
Dermot Bolger
Edward Bond
Bertolt Brecht
Howard Brenton
Anthony Burgess
Simon Burke
Jim Cartwright
Caryl Churchill
Complicite
Noël Coward
Lucinda Coxon
Sarah Daniels
Nick Darke
Nick Dear
Shelagh Delaney
David Edgar
David Eldridge
Dario Fo
Michael Frayn
John Godber
Paul Godfrey
David Greig
John Guare
Peter Handke
David Harrower
Jonathan Harvey
Iain Heggie
Declan Hughes
Terry Johnson
Sarah Kane
Charlotte Keatley
Barrie Keeffe

Howard Korder
Robert Lepage
Doug Lucie
Martin McDonagh
John McGrath
Terrence McNally
David Mamet
Patrick Marber
Arthur Miller
Mtwa, Ngema & Simon
Tom Murphy
Phyllis Nagy
Peter Nichols
Sean O'Brien
Joseph O'Connor
Joe Orton
Louise Page
Joe Penhall
Luigi Pirandello
Stephen Poliakoff
Franca Rame
Mark Ravenhill
Philip Ridley
Reginald Rose
Willy Russell
Jean-Paul Sartre
Sam Shepard
Wole Soyinka
Simon Stephens
Shelagh Stephenson
Peter Straughan
C. P. Taylor
Theatre Workshop
Sue Townsend
Judy Upton
Timberlake Wertenbaker
Roy Williams
Snoo Wilson
Victoria Wood

# Methuen Drama Classical Greek Dramatists

*Aeschylus Plays: One*
(Persians, Seven Against Thebes, Suppliants,
Prometheus Bound)

*Aeschylus Plays: Two*
(Oresteia: Agamemnon, Libation-Bearers, Eumenides)

*Aristophanes Plays: One*
(Acharnians, Knights, Peace, Lysistrata)

*Aristophanes Plays: Two*
(Wasps, Clouds, Birds, Festival Time, Frogs)

*Aristophanes & Menander: New Comedy*
(Women in Power, Wealth, The Malcontent,
The Woman from Samos)

*Euripides Plays: One*
(Medea, The Phoenician Women, Bacchae)

*Euripides Plays: Two*
(Hecuba, The Women of Troy, Iphigeneia at Aulis,
Cyclops)

*Euripides Plays: Three*
(Alkestis, Helen, Ion)

*Euripides Plays: Four*
(Elektra, Orestes, Iphigeneia in Tauris)

*Euripides Plays: Five*
(Andromache, Herakles' Children, Herakles)

*Euripides Plays: Six*
(Hippolytos, Suppliants, Rhesos)

*Sophocles Plays: One*
(Oedipus the King, Oedipus at Colonus, Antigone)

*Sophocles Plays: Two*
(Ajax, Women of Trachis, Electra, Philoctetes)

For a complete catalogue of Methuen Drama titles
write to:

Methuen Drama
36 Soho Square
London
W1D 3QY

or you can visit our website at:

www.methuendrama.com